THE EUROPEAN MONETARY SYSTEM

OTHER BOOKS BY PETER COFFEY

"European Monetary Integration" (with John R. Presley). Macmillan, London, 1971.

"The Social Economy of France", Macmillan, London, 1973.

"The World Monetary Crisis", Macmillan, London and St. Martin's Press, New York, 1974.

"The External Economic Relations of the EEC", Macmillan, London and St. Martin's Press, New York, 1976.

"Europe and Money", Macmillan, London and St. Martin's Press, New York, 1977.

"Economic Policies of the Common Market", Macmillan, London and St. Martin's Press, New York, 1979.

"The Common Market and its International Economic Policies", The Hague, 1982.

"Main Economic Policy Areas of the EEC", Martinus Nijhoff Publishers, The Hague, 1983.

"The European Monetary System – Past, Present and Future", Martinus Nijhoff Publishers, Dordrecht, 1984.

"The European Economic Community and Mexico" (edited, M.S. Wionczek (co-editor)), Martinus Nijhoff Publishers, 1987.

The European Monetary System – Past, Present and Future

SECOND REVISED EDITION

by

Dr. Peter Coffey

Europa Institute
University of Amsterdam
Amsterdam, The Netherlands

1987 **KLUWER ACADEMIC PUBLISHERS**
DORDRECHT / BOSTON / LANCASTER

Distributors

for the United States and Canada: Kluwer Academic Publishers, P.O. Box 358, Accord Station, Hingham, MA 02018-0358, USA
for the UK and Ireland: Kluwer Academic Publishers, MTP Press Limited, Falcon House, Queen Square, Lancaster LA1 1RN, UK
for all other countries: Kluwer Academic Publishers Group, Distribution Center, P.O. Box 322, 3300 AH Dordrecht, The Netherlands

Library of Congress Cataloging in Publication Data

Coffey, Peter.
The European monetary system--past, present, and future.

Includes bibliographical references and index.
1. Money--European Economic Community countries.
I. Title.
HG930.5.C63 1987 332.4'5'094 86-23833

ISBN-13: 978-94-010-8499-4 e-ISBN-13: 978-94-009-4488-6
DOI: 10.1007/978-94-009-4488-6

Notes about the Author

The author, a British national, is Head of the Economics Section of the Europa Instituut, University of Amsterdam. His main academic interests are in the field of European and international monetary economics and the Community's international economic and trading relations. Mr. Coffey, who speaks seven languages, has lectured in most countries of the European Economic Community as well as in many other parts of the world.

Notes about the Second Edition

A number of important structural changes have taken place in the European Monetary System (EMS) since the first edition of this work was published. Similarly, a number of profound proposals have been made for the future of the System. The author has therefore welcomed the publication of a second edition since it has given him the possibility of assessing all these changes and proposals in a special supplement which is placed at the end of the original text. Otherwise, only minor additions have been made to the text of the first edition.

Amsterdam, July, 1986.

LIST OF CONTENTS

LIST OF APPENDICES

LIST OF TABLES
and
DIAGRAMS

PREFACE

The European Monetary System (EMS) is perhaps the only success story of the Common Market since the First Enlargement. Its success, particularly where the commercial use of the ECU is concerned, has taken most experts by surprise. So much so, that when the author tried to recommend to his students a suitable and substantial work of study and/or reference about the experience of the EMS and its possible future evolution --- no book could be found. Thus, the author set out to write the present work.

The author's aim is not to give a historical account of the EMS. Rather, the intention is to place the experience in a major historical context wherein the System is seen an important transitional phase on the road to the implementation of a full economic and monetary union (EMU).

When examining the earlier plans for an EMU which saw the light of day between 1969 and 1970 (already so long ago!) clear reasons emerge why the original six founder Member States of the EEC should have found it logical to embark upon the road to an EMU - "provided the political will to do so existed". Thus, they had become highly integrated and were conducting half their trade with each other. Then, there was the desire to integrate still further ---- eventually leading (perhaps) to a political union. The existence of the Common Agricultural Policy (CAP) required stable (preferably fixed) exchange rates ---- an EMU would ensure just such a monetary stability. Last, but not least, the Community had become the world's most important commercial and trading bloc, holding enormous reserves of gold and hard currencies. It was therefore reasonable that the EEC should have a "common international monetary personality". The most concrete way of affirming such a personality would be to create a common currency.

Thus, many plans - representing the two main schools of economic and monetary thought (the "Economists" and the "Monetarists") - appeared, culminating in the compromise (second and definitive) Werner Plan. The main technical aspect of this plan was the so-called "Snake in the Tunnel", later becoming the simple "Snake Arrangement". This experiment, which lasted between 1972 and 1979, ended as a Deutsche-Mark Zone. It cannot be described as having been a great succes.

Already, however, in 1978, Chancellor Schmidt of West Germany and President Giscard d'Estaing of France, alarmed at American inaction in the monetary field and desirous of giving some momentum to further integration among Common Market countries, proposed a European Monetary System.

As is explained in this work, the EMS, which came into being in 1979, differs quite considerably from its predecessor. There are quite clear obligations imposed on the participants and they are under equally well defined constraints regarding intervention in the exchange markets and taking economic and monetary policy measures. On the other hand, it is much more flexible than the "Snake Arrangement". Exchange-rate adjustments (with one exception) have been swift, discrete and appropriate. The provision of credits for countries facing balance-of-payments problems is generous. Margins of fluctuations vis-ã-vis the ECU have been "individualised" for participating Member States. But, then the ECU is the kingpin of the System, and, to the author, this is what the future of the EMS is really all about.

Although this work does not include a section devoted to theory, theoretical considerations have, at all times, been actively present in the author's mind [1). In the case of the European Monetary System (EMS the author nevertheless considers, that, for the first time in many decades, the fundamental theory consideration, i.e. the question of public policy choice, to have been solved. Thus, all the participating countries in the EMS - plus the United Kingdom but not Greece (neither country being a member of the system) - have opted for the Magnifico[2)] definition of an optimum currency area (OCA) - i.e. "a similar propensity to inflate". This would appear to be a logical choice since the EMS is a de-facto monetary union, and, although in the short run a "portfolio approach" [3)] may be adopted by countries, in the medium - to long term, inflation rates must converge or something in the system (usually exchange rates) must give way. In contrast, where a full economic and monetary union (EMU) is concerned, current definitions of OCA's may not be valid --- indeed --- an OCA may not necessarily be an EMU!

To the author, then, the present economic target consensus among all but one of the EEC Member States is the correct one as far as the EMS is concerned. At the same time, the author considers the present system to be a transitional phase on the road to a full EMU. Furthermore, in advance of further moves towards greater economic and monetary integration certain areas should receive particular attention. These areas are specific technical considerations, the integration of capital markets and banking systems and the future "real" European Monetary Fund. Also, present national attitudes to the role of the ECU and the future Fund deserve special consideration. Therefore, in this work, the author, in contrast with a number of his colleagues, has devoted a major part of his studies to these specific questions.

After five years of activity and in strong contrast with its predecessor, the "Snake" Arrangement, the EMS may be said to have keen a success. Naturally, most of the system's protagonists would have wished to have seen a greater degree of integration materialise. Yet, not even the most ardent supporters of the EMS could have foreseen the ever increasing commercial use of the ECU. Furthermore, the author believes that the ECU's growing utilisation and success will force the Common Market to accept more integration and to create a "real" Fund.

Thus, this work is an advance study of areas where the author considers action will, by the force of events, have to be taken. The big question left unanswered in this book is when this action will be undertaken. Perhaps when the next edition of this work is published, this question will have been - at least partly - answered.

Amsterdam, June, 1984.

Notes:

1. A comprehensive examination of these theories may be found in P.Coffey, "Europe and Money", MacMillan, London, 1977.
2. See: G.Magnifico, "European Monetary Unification", MacMillan, London, 1973.
3. To the author, the "portfolio" approach means the willingness of institutes, banks and governments to hold the government paper of a country or countries.

Acknowledgements.

Although the interpretation of all the facts used in this book are the author's exclusive responsibility, it would not have been possible for him to have embarked upon this study without the kind and ready collaboration of colleagues and friends in different countries. He therefore wishes to thank everyone who has co-operated with him.

At the outset, a detailed questionnaire was sent to all the countries of the European Economic Community. In response to this, the author was kindly received by the Banque de France, in Paris, and he wishes to thank the following persons who were responsible for organising his visit and for furnishing him with information:
M. Alain Prate (Deputy Governor), M. Didier Bruneel (Director for Monetary Analysis and Statistics), Monsieur Penaud (Deputy Director for General Studies), M. Daniel Gabrielli (Deputy to the Director for Monetary Analysis and Statistics), Monsieur Leprou (Director for Foreign Studies) and M. M.F.Mazabraud (Head of Visits and Stages).

The following colleagues and friends furnished the author with information by post:
At the Deutsche Bundesbank, Dr.Heinrich Matthes (Director) and Dr. Klaus Weber. At the Bank of England, Mr. J.R.Hawkins and Mr. J.D.Ecklin. At the Banca d'Italia, Professor Giovanni Magnifico (Director - Stock Exchange Operations). At the Nederlandse Bank, Dr. Jan Koning (Head of Research) and Mr. J.P.Hogeweg (Assistant Chief - Domestic Research Department). At the Banque Nationale de Belgique, Mademoiselle Marie - Henriette Lambert, and, at the Commission de Banque, in Belgium, Mr. G.Gelders (Director). At the Danmark's National Bank, Mr. Erik Fossing Nielsen. At the Central Bank of Ireland, Mr. John P. O'Neill (Deputy Manager, International Relations Department). At the Institut Monétaire Luxembourgeois, the author received advice from M. Jean Guill (Directeur) and M. J.P.Schoder (Revisor).

The author is also grateful for discussions held with M. André Louw, Counsellor at the Commission of the European Communities, in Brussels, and with Paul Fabra, Le Monde, Paris.

Last, but by no means least, the author is particularly grateful to Mr. Ben Kotmans of the Europa Instituut, University of Amsterdam, who, with his customary good humour, patience and professional competence typed the manuscript of this work. Similarly, thanks are due to Mr. Matthijs van Blokland, a student assistant at the Europa Instituut, for his help in preparing the index to this book.

Special Note

Greece has not yet completed her transitional phase for her complete integration into the EEC (according to the rules of the Treaty of Rome). Equally, the Greek currency (the Drachma) will not be included in the ECU before the end of 1985. Also, Greece is not a member of the EMS. Therefore, the author did not include Greece in this study.

PART ONE: The Background to the European Monetary System.

Chapter 1. An Economic and Monetary Union : The Earlier Plans.

The real origins of the European Monetary System (hereafter called the EMS) go back as far as the end of the 1960's, when, at the end of 1969 in Den Haag, the Heads of the Member States of the European Economic Community agreed (provided the political will to do so existed) to move along the road to a full economic and monetary union (hereafter called an EMU).

This agreement was a rather momentous undertaking because a full EMU has the most profound economic and political implications for participating countries. Briefly, when speaking to non-economists, the author has explained an EMU as being the economic and monetary equivalent of a nation state. In the case of the members of a customs union, such as the EEC, a full EMU implies the free movement of goods, persons, capital and services within the union - plus the existence of a common external tariff vis-à-vis third parties. It implies irrevocably fixed exchange rates plus full convertibility - or a common currency. Also, it implies common economic, fiscal and monetary policies - together with a minimum degree of fiscal integration. In turn, common monetary policies vis-à-vis third parties would exist. Finally, these implications would presuppose certain common decision-making organs such as a central bank, among others, for example. Last, but by no means least, all this would imply a transfer of national sovereignty from the participating countries to the centre. Herein lies the real problem when nation states decide, on a voluntary basis, to move along the road to an EMU.

Why then, in 1969, did the original Six founder Member States of the European Economic Community take such a momentous decision? There were, in fact, a number of sound economic and structural reasons why such a decision seemed to be a reasonable one at that time. These countries, had, by 1968, achieved most of the aims as laid down in the Treaty of Rome. Quite simply, ahead of time, the customs union had been achieved. Consequently, the economies of the Member States had become well integrated and they were conducting about half their trade between themselves. Then, there was the position of the Community's Common Agricultural Policy (CAP). The successful functioning of this policy depended upon stable (preferably fixed) exchange rates. At an international level, the EEC had become the world's most important economic and trading bloc, endowed with the most important reserves of gold and convertible currencies. France had, for a number of years, considered that the Community should consequently be endowed with a "common international monetary personality". One of the best ways of demonstrating such a personality would be to create an EMU and a common currency. Finally, it should be borne in mind that up to 1968 the western world had experienced a full decade of relatively stable exchange rates. It was hoped that this situation would continue, and, one of the best ways of ensuring the continuation of this state of affairs would be to create an EMU.

The Original Plans for an EMU.

It is sometimes forgotten that no fewer than four different plans for an economic and monetary union within the EEC had been proposed during the period 1969-70 until the publication of the compromise (and second) Werner Plan in October 1970.[1)]

The afore-mentioned compromise plan was the result of the fundamental conflict between the two schools of thought, the Economists and the Monetarists. The former school mainly represented the official monetary views of West Germany and the Netherlands and the school's main architect was Herr Schiller. The latter school, the Monetarists, represented the official monetary views of France and Belgium and the school's main architects were Messieurs Barre and Giscard D'Estaing.

Basically, the differences between these two schools of thought concerned their attitudes to economic co-ordination and development, the fixing of exchange rates, the provision of credits for countries facing balance-of-payments problems, the liberalisation of capital movements, and the question of supranationality. In turn, these attitudes to a large degree reflected the economic and monetary experiences of the aforementioned countries since the end of the Second World War. Nevertheless, there was some degree of similarity in their attitudes towards budgetary harmonisation and co-ordination within the EEC.

Even thirteen years later, it is useful to examine in some detail the plans which represent most clearly the two schools of thought. These are the Schiller and the Second Barre Plans. Both are plans with far-reaching implications for an eventual EMU.

Turning first to the Schiller Plan, one notes that its overriding aim is the co-ordination of economic policies within the Community. Unfortunately, nowhere is it possible to find any clear guide as to how such co-ordination is to be realistically achieved. Also, it is difficult to see how some countries could liberalise capital movements without the provision of a well endowed monetary fund. Similarly, even in the more heady days of 1969 and 1970, it is hard to see France accepting with equanimity a transfer of sovereignty to central supranational organs of the Community. However, a high degree of economic convergence is a precondition for an EMU.

The Schiller Plan is divided as follows into four stages:

"1. The first stage is almost completely devoted to the setting-up of a concrete base for the co-ordination of economic policy. The principle here is the agreement on medium-term economic aims which should be checked each year by the Medium-term Economic Policy Committee. In this respect the Commission should recommend to member governments measures which should be adopted where the aims are not being achieved. Here, cyclical weapons should be developed and completed in each member state, allowing them to have the same effect in each country. To facilitate this process, economic statistics should be improved and co-ordinated and a communal system of economic signals should be organised.

In the strictly monetary sphere, at this stage, the holding of consultations regarding short-term measures plus the setting-up of short-term credits linked with demands in the field of economic policy co-ordination are proposed. Likewise the co-ordination of policy regarding rates of interest, under the aegis of the Council of Ministers and the governors of the Central Banks, is envisaged. Finally, at this stage, the capital markets of the Six should be gradually liberalised.

2. Having organised and co-ordinated economic policy weapons among the Six, Herr Schiller proposed the achievement of a more evenly balanced economic development as the main aim during the second stage. This would take the form of recommendations to be made by the Council of Ministers regarding the general economic trend of national budgets and the taking by the Council of more frequent and important decisions concerning economic policy. At the same time in the monetary field there should be more co-operation in the cadre of the committee of the governers of the Central Banks and of the monetary committee. Equally a system of medium-term monetary aid should be put into effect. By this time, approximately 1974-5, there should no longer exist any fundamental economic disequilibria between the member states.
3. At the third stage, measures of a supranational nature are proposed. These present an extraordinary volte-face with former German policy and mark a major divergence from the suggestions put forward by the Monetarists, who tend to reject supranational controls and to prefer the discipline of fixed exchange rates as the supreme measure of monetary control.

   Herr Schiller proposed an even stricter co-ordination of national economic priorities. In order to achieve this, the Community should be given powers which it does not yet possess. Thus the rule of the majority should be adopted as regards all important areas of economics, finance and money, e.g. control over national budgets. Hence the following steps should be taken: (a) a federal reserve system should be set up, based on the model of the United States; (b) the margins of exchange fluctuation between the national currencies should be reduced; (c) the exchange rates between the currencies of the member states should not be modified, except with the agreement of the other partners, using a system of qualified majority voting; (d) lastly, medium-term aid should be increased for members experiencing balance of payments difficulties and a European Reserve Fund should be set up.

Gradually, a portion of the national reserves should be transferred to this Fund.

4. The final stage would be that of total supranationality when all the necessary powers in the economic, financial and monetary fields would be transferred to the organs of the Community. The Committee of the governors of the Central Banks would become a European central council of banks using a majority voting system. Fixed and guaranteed exchange rates would be set between the member states, and at this final stage a single European unit of currency would be introduced."[2)]

In contrast, the Second Barre Plan, which represented both the views of the Commission as well as those of the Monetarists, and which was to have such an influence on the old 'Snake' System and on the present European Monetary System, was notable because it categorically rejected the principle of fluctuating exchange rates and because it wished to give a unified international monetary personality to the European Economic Community. The main reasons given for the rejection of fluctuating exchange rates is that such fluctuations would hinder the desired convergence of the different national economies, would hinder the creation of a Community capital market and would have negative social and psychological effects on the EEC. As a satisfactory move in the direction of fixing exchange rates, it is proposed that the margin of parity between the national currencies of the Member States of the Common Market should be reduced from 1.5 to 1.0 per cent. Although, like the Schiller Plan, the Barre Plan does set down a series of stages for the achievement of a full economic and monetary union, it, unwisely, unlike its rival plan, sets down a time table for this task. Here, again, this was to be a less than happy influence on the definitive Werner Plan.

The stages of the Second Barre Plan are as follows:

"1. In the first stage (1970-1) the provision of medium-term aid (using the S.D.R.'s), as proposed in the First Plan, is suggested. By the end of 1970 the third economic medium-term plan should be adopted and economic policies should be more effectively co-ordinated, including medium-term budgetary policy with annual meetings of the Finance Ministers from 1971 onwards. At this stage, moves should also be made to generalise the value-added tax (V.A.T.) and plans set up to

harmonise its levels throughout the EEC. Similar measures should also be adopted regarding capital movements within the Community. Under the aegis of the governors of the Central Bank, moves should be made towards the harmonisation of credit policy.
At the international level, the Community should make clear its position in the monetary sphere and establish rules regarding exchange-rate-fluctuations between the EEC and third parties.

2. During the second phase (1972-5) - the decisive stage - general economic policy directives should be laid down at Community level and its economic evolution should be examined each year on a 'rolling' basis.
Budgetary and fiscal policies should be harmonised, particularly the levels of the V.A.T., and all states should use similar budgetary weapons. Interestingly enough, M.Barre suggested that the main economic, fiscal and monetary lines should be examined at regular intervals by the Commission in consultation with the social partners and representatives of economic and social life.
The Community capital market should be organised, thus removing the necessity of its access to the 'international' capital market.
Already by the beginning of 1972, exchange fluctuations between the members' currencies should not be greater than 1 per cent, and in 1973 with the new allocation of S.D.R.'s these units should be communally controled.

3. Thus, after an examination by the Commission of the situation in 1975, the Council could decide whether to move on to the third stage in 1976 or in 1978. At this stage the organs of the Community should be endowed with all the powers which an economic and monetary union would necessitate. A council of governors of the Central Banks should be set up to create a communal banking system. A European Reserve Fund should be set up. In two stages, all fluctuations between currency parities should be irrevocably eliminated.
Capital, should be allowed to circulate freely within the Community, taxes should be harmonised, and finally a European unit of currency would be created." [3)]

The next plan, the First Werner Report, which was examined by the Community Finance Ministers in Venice in May 1970, was only concerned with the initial stage of integration, 1971-4. During the course of the examination by the ministers, there seemed to be some consensus of opinion about the reduction of the margin of fluctuation around the parities of EEC national currencies, but a profound difference of opinion over the setting-up of a Reserve Fund during the first stage of the EMU.

It was grave difference of opinion between the representatives of the two schools of thought at Venice in May and then in Luxemburg in June, 1970, which forced M.Barre to intervene on behalf of the Commission to ask the Ministers to vote on certain points on which they agreed and to ask the Werner Committee to prepare a final report for the Autumn in which the differences of opinion in other fields would be reduced to a minimum.

Thus, the Second and definitive Werner Plan [4)] was the compromise between these two schools of thought and because the blueprint for the first stage of the EMU, better known as the "Snake" System.

Although the definitive Werner Plan was a compromise between the two schools of thought, it did, nevertheless, err somewhat more on the side of the Monetarists than on that of the Economists. This leaning is shown in proposal for the narrowing of the margin of fluctuation around the central parity of the national currencies of the participating EEC Member States.

The Report only made detailed proposals for the first stage of the EMU (1971-1973), but, did draw the attention of the ministers to certain problems such as the regional one and the dangerous possibility of certain central banks losing out through exchange-rate intervention. In the latter case, it was even suggested that compensation should be arranged.

However, the Committee of Governors of Central Banks (annex no.5. of the Report) appeared to have been blind to the fact of the crumbling nature of the international monetary edifice since they continued to give far too great an importance to the role of the US dollar. Similarly, they were short-sighted in their lack of support for the provision of substantial credits for countries facing balance-of-payments problems -

suggesting that deficits and surpluses would simply balance themselves out!

Chapter 2. The Experience of the "Snake" System.

The "Snake" System in Operation.

The real technical manifestation of the System was to be the "Snake in the Tunnel". This "Snake" was to have been a narrow band of fluctuation (of 1.2 per cent) originally planned for the central parities of the national currencies of the participating Member States of the EEC - which was to have moved in the wider band of fluctuation (1.5 per cent) formerly allowed for the US dollar (see: diagram No.1). However, following the major dollar crisis of 1971, the suspension of dollar convertibility against gold and the subsequent Smithonian Agreement allowing a margin of fluctuation around the dollar of 4.5 per cent, the EEC had to re-examine the situation. Therefore, in March 1971, it was agreed to introduce, on an experimental basis, before 1 July 1972 (in fact this was introduced on 24 April 1972) a System whereby the margin of fluctuation around the currencies of the participating EEC Member States would be 2.25 per cent - this was to move in a dollar tunnel of 4.5 per cent (see: diagram No.2). But, with the complete floating of the dollar in March 1973, the tunnel was dropped and the "Snake" participants organised a joint float against the dollar.

Although the "Snake" System did constitute a zone of monetary stability in a sea of considerable international upheavals, it was not a particularly happy experience (see: Appendix No.1). Both the United Kingdom and the Republic of Ireland left the arrangement after participating in it for just under two months. Italy left a few months later. France left temporarily, returned and then definitively left the Arrangement. At the end of its life (March 1979) the "Snake" Arrangement represented a Deutsche Bank Zone, consisting of Belgium, Denmark, Luxembourg, the Netherlands and West Germany.

Many reasons may be advanced for the relative failure of this first attempt at creating an EMU within the EEC. By its very nature, the "Snake" Arrangement, being an attempt at stabilising exchange-rates, was sailing against international economic and monetary winds as symbolised by an international system of floating exchange rates. This situation made a high degree of co-ordination of national economic and monetary policies among the participating countries absolutely essential. In reality, such co-ordination was non-existant. In exchange for a greater degree of economic and monetary self-discipline among these states, a much more substantial amount of credits should have been made available to participating countries facing balance-of-payments problems. The plight of both the United Kingdom and Italy made such a need obvious. In contrast, the technical mechanism was both too rigid and one-sided. When exchange-rate adjustments were accepted - they normally came too late. Also, the responsibility for making national economic adjustments - as well as for exchange-rate intervention - tended to fall much more heavily on the deficit countries (balance-of-payments) than on the surplus ones. Nevertheless, the System did represent a rare zone of monetary stability.

As the system was approaching its demise, two very serious developments were making themselves manifest at the international level. One was the inflation-creating element embodied in floating exchange rates. The other was the glaring lack of monetary action by the American Administration concerning the US dollar. Both these developments considerably alarmed Governments of EEC Member States - especially those of France and West Germany.

The first semi-official call for united Community action to these two developments came in a speach made by Mr.Jenkins (then, Head of the EEC Commission) at Florence, in October 1977, when he made a proposal for a European Monetary System. This idea was taken up at the Bremen Summit in July 1978 - especially by Chancellor Schmidt and President Giscard D'Estaing. The EMS came into operation on 13 March 1979.

The "Snake" in the tunnel arrangement as proposed in the Werner plan in 1970.

DIAGRAM No.1

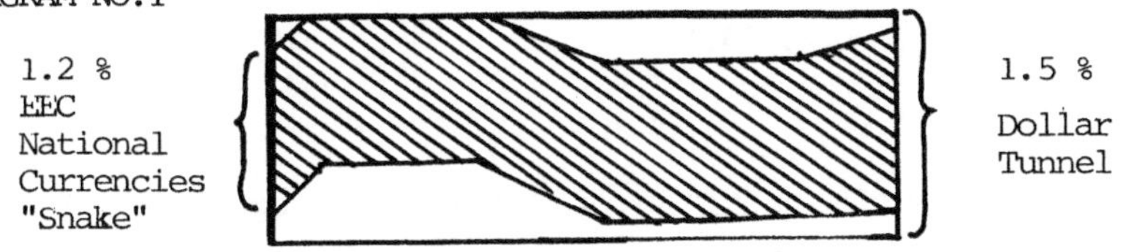

DIAGRAM No.2

The proposed "Snake" in the tunnel arrangement following the Smithsonion agreements in 1971.

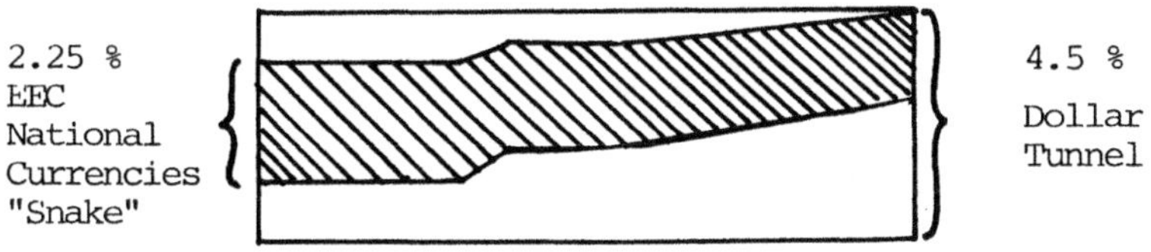

Reproduced from: P.Coffey, "Main Economic Policy Areas of the EEC", Nijhoff, Den Haag, 1983.

NOTES: Part One.

1. A full examination of these plans may be found in Part Two of "European Monetary Integration", P.Coffey and J.R.Presley, Macmillan, London, 1971.

2 en 3.

Quoted from Part Two, "European Monetary Integration", P.Coffey and J.R.Presley, Macmillan, London, 1971.

4. Council - Commission of the European Communities. "Report to the Council and to the Commission on the Realisation by Stages of Economic and Monetary Union in the Community" (The 'Werner Report'), Luxembourg, October 1970.

PART TWO: The European Monetary System.

Chapter 3. The Reasons for the System.

At the end of the last chapter, reference was made to the growing disenchantment with the inflationary effects of floating exchange rates and with the alarm at the lack of action in the monetary field by the U.S. Administration. This latter point was really important. The economies of the EEC Member States are either open or very open ones (see: table No. 1) whereas those of both the United States and the Soviet Union are closed ones - exporting only about 5 per cent of their gross national product. Therefore, in contrast with the Americans, the West Europeans just cannot afford to ignore volatile and violent exchange rate movements. Consequently, they just had to do something about the lack of American action.

At this point, the question should be asked, why did not the Common Market countries simply organise a joint float against the U.S. dollar? The answer to this question must be that the West Germans and the French - in the persons of Chancellor Schmidt and President Giscard D'Estaing - wanted something more than a simple arrangement vis-à-vis the Americans. They preferred a move towards a greater degree of economic and political integration in the Community. The decision to create a European Monetary System (hereafter called the E.M.S.) was much more a political than an economic one.

The Deutsche Bundesbank (the West German Central Bank), which, contrary to its constitutional right, was not adequately consulted about the System, has always been strongly opposed to the EMS. In 1982, it voiced profound objections to any moves towards a second stage of the System. The Bank's objections to the EMS are based on the fears of increasing inflation through the creation of extra Deutsche-Marks necessitated by exchange rate intervention.

TABLE No.1.

EEC : Degree of "Open-ness" in National Economies in 1982.

(as a percentage of GNP)

	Exports	Imports
Belgium	64.0	68.4
Denmark	36.8	36.3
France	22.2	24.0
Germany (West)	29.5	28.7
Greece	14.7	26.4
Ireland	53.2	68.1
Italy	24.7	28.2
Netherlands	58.9	54.9
United Kingdom	27.1	23.9
EEC Total	29.9	30.1

Source: EEC Commission, "European Economy", No.12, July 1982.

Italy, although at all times in favour of European economic and political integration, had suspicions about the apparent Franco-German co-operation. Eventually, the Italians were placated by the special wide band of fluctuation for the Lira which they obtained. Also, like the Irish, they obtained interest rate subsidies.

The smaller countries, Denmark and the Benelux States, at all times closely linked economically to West Germany and the Deutsche Mark, always tended to follow the movements of that currency.

Even more so than Italy, the United Kingdom was deeply suspicious of the foregone agreement between France and Germany. The British had also never forgotten the trauma of their disastrous experience in the old "Snake" Arrangement, when, in the space of less than two months, they lost about 30 per cent of their reserves. Furthermore, since the Pound Sterling was now an oil currency - and tending to appreciate - there were sound scientific reasons why the British should not join the EMS.

At a more profound level, there were reasons linked with the traditions of national economic philosophy which made the planned EMS attractive. France, with the notable exception of the period 1945-1957, had, since the beginning of the century, been in favour of stable exchange rates. Thus, any agreement or system which aimed at stabilising exchange rates should find favour with French governments - especially with a liberal economic one.

West Germany, obsessed with the memories of the dreadful economic and political consequences of the two periods of inflation in the 1920's and the 1930's, had made the control of inflation its main postwar economic and monetary aim. Here, any system aiming at controlling inflation would tend to be supported by a West German Government.

Certain of the smaller countries, notably the Benelux ones, had also, since the end of the Second World War, tended to prone economic and monetary policies aiming at stable exchange rates and the control of inflation. These countries also, at least officially, tended to favour a greater degree of European economic and political integration. Thus, systems which embodied these aims would tend to be supported by these countries.

At this point, it is possible to observe certain economic, monetary and political trends and preferences among the majority of Community Member States. There is a general alarm at the collapse of the US dollar and the inaction of the US Administration in the monetary field. This alarm is reinforced by the fears (expressed by all EEC countries) of inflation and the desire to combat this danger.

The desire for stable exchange rates and to combat inflation conforms with the basic economic and monetary philosophy of at least five Member States. Some of these countries also desire to see a greater degree of economic and political integration in the EEC. Thus, the stage is set for the construction of a system which has to be superior to the old "Snake" Arrangement.

However, it is essential to bear in mind that the EMS is essentially a political decision taken under the impetus of France and West Germany. It obviously has to be more flexible and compulsory than its predecessor. Furthermore, a new failure would tend to bring discredit on any future attempts at economic and monetary integration.

Chapter 4. The Mechanisms of the System.

The European Monetary System, which came into being on 13 March, 1979, clearly demonstrated - both in the Resolution of the Council of Ministers of 5 December 1978 - as well as in the mechanisms used in the System - fundamental economic and monetary aims which had been missing from its predecessor. Thus, the author discerns the following aims in the EMS:

(i) a greater degree of convergence of the economies of the participating Member States,

(ii) the adoption of a common public policy choice for these countries - more specifically - the control of levels of inflation - also aiming at convergence,

(iii) exchange-rate stability,

(iv) the promotion of a central role for the ECU, and,

(v) hopefully some moves to a greater degree of integration among the Community's Member States.

Clearly had the old Snake Arrangement mechanism of a common band for currency to currency ("GRID") fluctuation simply been adopted - the EMS would not have differed from its predecessor. However, in view of the afore-mentioned aims which the author finds to be inherent in the System, then a more sophisticated, effective and responsible mechanism had to be devised. It had to embody these qualities, constraints and indeed flexibility which had been missing from its predecessor.
Equally, it had to attempt to share the responsibilities for exchange-rate intervention between both the surplus and deficit countries. Then, the ECU, had, technically at least, to become the kingpin of the mechanism. Equally, for exchange rate intervention purposes

more sophisticated, effective and responsible mechanisms had to be invented. The outcome is two bands of fluctuation running side by side. The first is indeed the old national currency to national currency (or "GRID") mechanism whereby a band of fluctuation (as was formerly the case with the "Snake" System) 2.25 per cent (with a band of 6 per cent allowed for Italy) operates. However, alongside this band a much more effective ECU - national currency band of fluctuation operates. Here, the Commission has introduced a most novel system. This is the "individualisation" of the band of fluctuation for each participating currency (see: diagram No.3). This was necessary in order to prevent certain currencies from coming under unwarranted pressure on the exchange markets. At the same time, this mechanism was further refined by the very important introduction of a "divergence" threshold, the equivalent of 75 per cent of the central part of the "individualisation", at which point, the country concerned should take action to bring its currency into line.

Here, the responsibilities of the country concerned when the Divergence Indicator is reached vis-à-vis the ECU by its currency are clearly laid down by the Resolution of the Council of Ministers of 5 December 1978. There are: " - diversified intervention,

- monetary measures,
- drawing on credit facilities, and
- external and domestic policy measures ".

Another major innovation of the EMS is the important place given to the ECU[2]. The idea here is that the Community's unit-of-account (used for all official EEC transactions) should be the king pin for the future moves towards the implementation of an economic and monetary union. The hoped-for means of achieving this aim was to have been through a transformation of the European Fund for Monetary Co-operation (at present a shadow of a legal entity) into a more concrete organ at a second stage in the evolution of the EMS. To this end, the participating Member States, together with the United Kingdom, which is not a member of the EMS, have exchanged 20 per cent of their holdings of gold and dollars against the ECU's.

The lack of credits under the old "Snake" System was one of its more serious defects. This important defect has been largely made good under the EMS. Thus, the amount of credits available to Member States - should they face pressures on their currencies and balance-of-payments problems - are substantially larger. In 1981, the approximate value of these credits[3)] was 25 billion units of account as compared with 11.45 billion units of account under the former system.

A further refinement of the System was the setting-aside each year for a period of five years - until 1983 - of 200 million ECU's to provide interest subsidies on EIB or NCI loans for Italy and Ireland.

To the unitiated outside observer, the sharing of the responsibilities for the management of the EMS may, at first sight, seem to be unduly complex. In reality, this sharing is purely a reflection of the difficult process of economic, monetary and political integration.

The actual responsibility for the day-to-day intervention in the money markets to keep national currences within the agreed bands of fluctuation naturally lies with the central banks of the participating Member States. However, the overall responsibility for the management of the EMS lies with the Commission. Furthermore, this same body has the right to make recommendations about national economicand monetary policy matters to the same countries. This right emanates from the decision of the Council of Ministers concerning the attainment of a high degree of convergence of the economic policies of the Member States, taken in February 1974.

Officially and legally speaking, the swaps of 20 per cent of national holdings of gold and dollars against ECU's on a 3-monthly rolling basis[4)], made by nine Member States, were with the European Fund for Monetary Co-operation. However, this institution is only a legal fiction consisting of a name-plate on a building in Luxembourg[5)]. Thus, the swaps, like the short- and medium-term credits, are in fact managed by the Bank for International Settlements (B.I.S.), in Basel, in Switzerland. The only precondition here is that the two or three officials managing these matters should be Community nationals.

DIAGRAM No. 3.

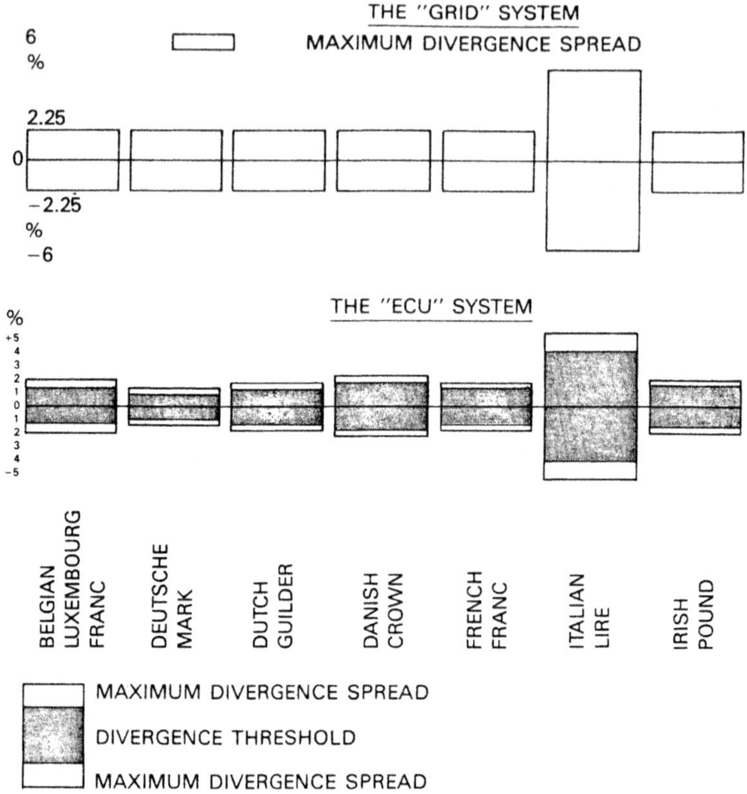

DIVERENCE THRESHOLD

When a currency reaches the upper or lower limits of this band, the Government concerned must intervene in the exchange markets.

Reproduced from: The European Monetary System - Six Months Later.
P.Coffey, Three Banks Review, December '79, London.

TABLE No.2.

The Commission's "individualisation" of Maximum Divergence Spreads and Divergence Thresholds.

Currencies	Maximum Divergence Spread vis-à-vis the ECU %	Divergence Threshold vis-à-vis the ECU %
Belgian/Luxembourg Franc	2.03	1.52
Deutsche Mark	1.51	1.13
Dutch Guilder	2.01	1.51
Danish Crown	2.18	1.64
French Franc	1.80	1.35
Italian Lira	5.43	4.07
Irish Pound	2.22	1.67
Pound Sterling	-	-

Lastly, whilst short-term credits are accorded to Member States on an automatic basis, such is not the case with medium-term ones. Here, the Council of Ministers (advised by the Commission) makes policy recommendations to the country or the countries receiving aid. Equally, where the Community floats loans on the international market on behalf of Member States, the Council attaches policy conditions to such help.

Doubtless, the making of such policy conditions should provide a possible means of, to some degree, at least, co-ordinating national economic policies ---- and even of leading to greater integration among Community Member States. However,(as was criticised in the Commission's 1983 statement to the Council on Financial Integration, see: Appendix IV), it is precisely such recourse to Community financial support that ountries have tried to avoid since 1977. Instead, they prefer to use "safeguard" clauses and thereby re-impose controls over capital movements wherever they face balance-of-payments and similar problems. This is clearly not a satisfactory situation and causes the Community to move backwards rather than forwards. Despite this disappointing record, the author is somewhat optimistic about the future. On the one hand, a major change in policy was French recourse, in 1983, to a very important Community loan - rather than going to non-EEC sources. On the other hand, as inflation rates among countries converge - which is now the tendency among Western countries - it will be possible to liberalise capital movements. This, however, is a major subject which is examined in greater detail later in this work.

Chapter 5. The System in Operation.

At this point in this work, it is useful to examine the record of the European Monetary System. However, this record should be placed in its proper context. This implies that we are not examining an EMU - but an EMS - which is a kind of de-facto monetary union. Then, it is important to bear in mind the outside pressures - as well as the inside ones - which have been challenges to the System. To the author, basically four main questions should be asked when assessing the record of the EMS. These are:

(i) has the System constituted a zone of relative monetary stability?

(ii) have adjustments in exchange rates taken place easily and discreetly?

(iii) have inflation rates tended to converge among the participating countries?

(iv) are participating countries applying rigorous economic and monetary policies which they might not have applied had they not been members of the EMS?

In answering the first question, the record of the EMS should be placed in the context of the steep and rapid changes in the values of the Yen and the US Dollar in the foreign exchange markets. In comparison with these violent movements and pressures, the EMS has constituted a zone of monetary stability.

This good record, with the exception of the most recent adjustment, is also the answer to the second question. Adjustments (see: Appendix No.II) particularly when compared with the "Snake" Arrangement, have tended to be swift, discreet and relevant. In this sense, the System has proved to be a flexible one. In the case of the most recent adjustment, the pending elections in West Germany and France made a timely change in the exchange rates unacceptable to both countries. Therefore, pressure was allowed to build up on the Deutsche Mark and the French Franc, and, the eventual discussions which took place concerning the degree of adjustment were so heated and protracted that the EMS was, in effect, suspended for a day.

Turning to the third question, the situation is less satisfactory. In the majority of cases, inflation rates have fallen, but, the gap between the West German rates and those of the other participating countries has remained.

The last and fourth question may be answered in the affirmative. All the participating Member States wish to remain in the System. This implies the taking of internal economic and monetary measures as well as exchange rate adjustments. In the case of France, in 1982, the Government made a volte-face with the initial expansionary economic policy of President Mitterand. The severity of these new policies was increased in 1983. In Belgium, the Government, having obtained the right to introduce economic measures by decree, applied severe policies in 1982 which appeared to bear fruit in 1983, when the Belgian Franc was re-adjusted upwards - having previously been devalued - for the first time in thirty years.

Similar restrictive policies are being adopted in Denmark, the Netherlands and in the Republic of Ireland. Even the United Kingdom, which is not a participant in the EMS, continues to adopt deflationary policies. Only in Italy do the budgetary deficits remain unacceptably and inflationary levels remain unacceptably high.

Other Considerations.

Two other aims of the EMS were the greater use of national EEC currencies (rather than the US Dollar which was the currency of intervention under the "Snake" Arrangement) in intervening in the exchange markets and a greater use of the ECU within the European Economic Community.

Regarding the first of these two aims, a curious and mixed situation has developed. When it was logical and desirable for countries to use Community national currencies it was not always possible for these states to obtain the desired currencies in the quantities and with the speed which were necessary. This must be seen as a technical defect of the EMS. Then there was the fundamental problem of the appreciation of the US Dollar which consequently necessitated a use of this currency in the

TABLE No.3.

EEC : Price Changes : Annual Percentage Rates of Change.

Consumer Prices

(change over Previous Year)

	1979	1980	1981
Belgium	3.9	6.5	7.6
Denmark	9.6	11.5	10.7
France	10.9	13.2	12.5
Germany (West)	4.0	5.3	5.9
Greece	17.7	23.7	24.4
Ireland	13.4	18.3	20.5
Italy	15.0	20.4	19.0
Netherlands	4.3	6.6	6.7
United Kingdom	14.3	15.5	10.7

Source: Eurostat and EEC Commission, "European Economy", No.12, July 1982.

exchange markets (generally implying the sales thereof).

In contrast, the experience of the ECU has been one of the success stories of the EMS. Writing in 1982, the author declared that the "ECU was foredoomed to be successful". These words have been borne out. The ECU is the official unit-of-account of the Community. Also, largely as a result of the exchange of 20 per cent of their holdings of gold and dollars by 9 of the Member States with the European Fund for Monetary Co-operation (hereafter referred to as the EFMC) in exchange for ECU's there were at the end of 1982 approximately 42 billion ECU's in existence. In this sense, the ECU is the second most important international monetary reserve asset. Also the private use of this unit of account has increased. In June, 1983, three countries, Belgium, France and Italy, allowed private accounts to be held in ECU's. According to the Morgan Guaranty Trust, in 1982, ECU-bonds reached the third position in the new eurobond issues by currency of denomination after the US Dollar and the Deutsche Mark (see: Table No.4.)

According to the author, this increased use of the ECU will most probably lead to the EFMC being transformed into a "real" and living organ. It had been hoped that the EMS would enter upon a second stage of development in March 1981 - implying a transformation of the EFMC. However, for a mixture of reasons, this hope did not materialise. A year later, the Deutsche Bundesbank voiced strong objections to either a move of the System to a more advanced stage of development or to any transfer of real responsibility to the EFMC.

The author's hopes concerning the future are based on the following premise. The ECU, backed by the economic, commercial and political strength of the Community is bound to succeed. Further, it is a very good risk spreader. Gradually, more businessmen and private citizens will bring pressure to bear on their governments to allow them the right to hold private ECU banking accounts. The author then assumes that EEC Governments, unwilling to countenance a repetition of the experience of the Euro-dollar market - which is outside their control - will prefer to keep control of the ECU market. Logically, the most effective means of keeping control of this market would be to transfer

TABLE No. 4

New Eurobond Issues

(New Issues each year in millions of dollars)

	1981	1982
U.S.Dollar	26,830	42,930
Deutsche Mark	1,277	2,487
ECU	309	1,301
Canadian Dollar	634	1,181
Others	2,037	1,298
Total	31,616	49,839

Source: Morgan Guaranty Trust, World Financial Markets, February 1983.
Quoted from: ECU Newsletter, February 1983.

control thereof to a transformed EFMC.

Final Observations.

The record of the EMS to date has been a mixed one - which errs clearly on the positive rather than on the negative side. As such, it is in all respects vastly superior to the old "Snake" Arrangement.

Thus, on the positive side, one may observe that the EMS has been a zone of stability in a very stormy international monetary sea. With one exception, exchange-rate adjustments have been discreet and swift ..... and generally appropriate in magnitude. Also, nearly all the participating Member States are currently taking economic and monetary measures to bring their inflationary rates down. Similarly, the use of the ECU has progressed quite substantially.

On the negative side, one may observe that the Community has failed to move on to a second stage of the EMS - as had been hoped for at its inception. This is an important defect. Then, in contrast to the increase in the use of ECU's, there have been shortages of EC national currencies on occasions when needed for exchange-rate intervention.

Although the vast majority of the participating Member States are trying to bring inflation rates down, the gaps between them do remain. And, it must be observed that co-ordinating economic and monetary policies of a supernational nature do not exist.

Having made these observations, it is important to point out that despite the grave economic and monetary problems experienced by some Member States - notably France and Italy - no country has left the EMS. This is indeed a notable difference with its predecessor.

Regarding the future, it seems that action should be taken concerning the use of the ECU, the provision of national currencies for exchange intervention purposes, the more effective co-ordination of economic and monetary policies and the integration of the banking systems and capital markets. Last but not least, steps should be taken to transform the present somewhat embryonic European Fund for Monetary Co-operation into a real European Monetary Fund.

NOTES : Part Two.

1. All the EEC Member States - except Greece and the United Kingdom - participate in the EMS. However, Britain has participated in the "swap" operation - exchanging 20 per cent of its holding of gold and dollars against ECU's.

2. The composition of the ECU, as calculated on 28 June 1974, is as follows:

0.828	Deutsche Mark	3.66	Belgian Francs
0.0885	Pound Sterling	0.14	Luxembourg Francs
1.15	French Francs	0.217	Danish Crown
109.00	Italian Lira	0.00759	Irish Pound
0.286	Dutch Guilders		

3. The new credits are divided as follows: 14 billion ECU's in short term and 11 billion ECU's in medium-term credit. A short term credit is available for a maximum period of 9 months and a medium-term one for between 3 and 5 years.

4. This formula was adopted in order to leave the ownership of these reserves in the hands of the Member States.

5. This situation exists because in 1973, no decision could be made about the location of the final home for this institution - the contestants being Luxembourg and London.

PART THREE : The Future of the EMS : Technical Considerations.

The future of the EMS really revolves around the question as how far the participating Member States wish the System to develop into a full economic and monetary union. Should their preference extend no further than the maintenance of the present quasi-monetary union, they may well decide not to make any further technical and institutional changes to the System. However, should this be their wish, the author suspects that the inevitable future development in the use of the ECU may well force them to take some decisions. Should they wish to move to a more advanced stage of development, specific plans should be prepared in the very near future. There are already clear areas of activity where action is desirable. The main areas are the role of the ECU and the further convergence of national economic and monetary policies.

Chapter 6. The Future Role of the ECU.

In 1981[1], the author defined the optional roles of a currency and a reserve asset as the following:

(i) a unit of account,

(ii) a medium of exchange (between individuals),

(iii) a means of settlement (between institutes, central banks, governments and similar bodies),

(iv) a store of value, and,

(v) a refuge from economic and/or political instability. In this last case, individuals and/or institutes may be willing to forego (at least partially and/or temporarily)the attractiveness of the role of the currency or asset as a store value (iv) in exchange for enhanced security.

When assessing the degree to which the ECU fulfills these five roles, one finds that it fares extremely well. In fact, it fulfills all these functions. The only proviso concerns the second function, since, at the time of writing (June 1983) only four EEC Member States actively encourage the private use of ECU's either through the opening of private ECU denominated bank accounts or through the procurement of credits (loans) denominated in ECU's.

Legally speaking, the ECU is recognized as a foreign currency by all EEC countries, except in Greece, Ireland and West Germany. Basically speaking, this fact should mean that it should be possible for all residents and non-residents to hold private ECU-denominated bank accounts in seven of the EEC countries. In practice, however, the situation is somewhat different. Thus, in Italy, Belgium and Luxembourg, both residents and non-residents alike, may hold ECU accounts. In France, both residents and non-residents may receive credits denominated in ECU's.

Since the Netherlands, Denmark and the United Kingdom all recognise the ECU as a foreign currency, it is legally possible to keep accounts in ECU's (though, in Denmark, this would be for residents only). In reality, in the Netherlands, not all commercial banks appear to be aware of the legal right to open ECU accounts. In the United Kingdom, the private use of ECU's is neither encouraged nor restricted - consequently, few people in Britain appear to be aware of the existence of the ECU! In Denmark, the situation appears to be somewhat the same as in the Netherlands. In West Germany, the opening of private bank accounts in ECU's is forbidden.

Although, like the Germans, the Greeks and Irish do not recognise the ECU as a foreign currency, nevertheless, on occasions, transfers of large amounts on ECU's (e.g. from the European Regional Fund and the European Investment Bank) have been made through the banks of these last two countries.

Thus, in practice, it would appear that in four countries, Italy, France, Belgium and Luxembourg, the use of the ECU is actively encouraged. In Denmark, the Netherlands and the United Kingdom, the ECU is recognised as a foreign currency and it is therefore possible - but not always easy - to open ECU bank accounts there. The Greeks, Irish and West

Germans do not recognise the ECU as a foreign currency - therefore, in principle it is not possible to open ECU bank accounts in these countries. In reality, in West Germany, the practice is forbidden, whereas in Ireland and Greece, where large amounts of ECU's are involved, the necessary bank transfers would be allowed.

This present state of affairs, regarding the private use of the ECU, is clearly not satisfactory since it being more and more used in other spheres. It is the unit of account for all the official transactions of the Community. An every increasing number of Euro-bond issues are being floated in ECU's.
Consequently, the ECU is the third most important currency/reserve asset for the European Investment Bank (EIB) and for Italy. Internationally, it is among the top three currencies and reserve assets. Therefore, the author proposes that all the Community Member States should agree to allow their citizens to hold private bank accounts in ECU's.

Similarly, another issue of ECU's should be organised. The next issue should not only include gold and dollars, but also national currencies. Eventually, half of the currencies circulating inside the EEC might be ECU's because half of the trade of the Common Market is internal. Since, however, the realisation of such an aim would take time, a more urgent and practical intermediate aim would be the use of the ECU by a considerably strengthened EFMC in the exchange markets to relieve national Member State currencies of pressures .... particularly of pressures against the US dollar.
Pertinent proposals in this sense have been made by Giovanni Magnifico. Also, as the Commission has proposed (see: Appendix III), Community central banks should be allowed to settle up to 100 per cent of their debts in ECU's - instead of 50 per cent as is presently the case.
The reasons for the great attractiveness of the commercial use of the ECU in some countries are mainly twofold. First, its rates are lower than those at which the local/national currency may be borrowed. Second, unlike the Euro-dollars, for example, the ECU is a foreign currency over which the local government has control. Equally, at a commercial level, the ECU is attractive because it is supported by the economic weight

of the EEC - the world's main economic trading bloc - and in its quality as a risk spreader. Mainly for these reasons, its use is likely to increase - whether or not individual Common Market national Governments approve of this fact. Therefore, it seems highly desirable that careful preparations should be made in advance of this materialising.

It is also most important that the control of the developing ECU Bond market should be under Community control. Preferably, the situation of the Euro-dollar market - with all the implications of lack of Community control - should not be allowed to be repeated in the case of the ECU Bond market.

Other Possibilities.

There exist other very important roles which the ECU might play. One role, which both Giovanni Magnifico and the author have advocated for over a decade is its use with travellers' cheques. At the time of writing, it is most reassuring to note that a group of French banks - together with the Société Française de Chèque de Voyage - are in the process of creating a company which will study and develop a travellers' cheque denominated in ECU's[2)]. Such progress will be something of a landmark for the inhabitants of the EEC, because, hitherto, particularly in the monetary field with all its technicalities and complexities, the main criticism levelled at the Community by its citizens is its remoteness, and, with the exception of the price of agricultural products, its apparent irrelevance to everyday life.

The other major role - which will be examined in greater depth and detail later in this book - is the use of the ECU as an international reserve currency by non Community countries. Here, some experts would see this role as being particularly relevant for the states with which the EEC has majory economic links. More immediately, attention is being directed to this particular role being used in the Community's relations with Third World countries. The example to which reference is made in this context is France's support for the Franc used in trade between Francophone countries in Africa. (these two zones are L'Afrique Centrale, UMAC; and the Union Monétaire de L'Afrique de L'Ouest, UMOA).

Further Technical Considerations concerning the ECU.

There are a few other technical considerations which deserve further examination when assessing the future role of the ECU. One of these is the observation that, in reality, there exist two ECU's. One, which the author calls the "official" ECU, is composed of all the EEC currencies (with, until 1985, the exception of the Greek Drachma). This "official" unit of account is that which is used in all the Community's official transactions, e.g. in the allocation of development of regional and social aid. But, there also exists (though officially never admitted as such) an "EMS" ECU, which, not only excludes the Greek Drachma, but also the Pound Sterling.

This observation would seem to confirm the possibility (as was formerly the case) of different kinds of ECU existing side by side.

The most important technical consideration concerning the future of the ECU is its intermediate role within the EEC as a parallel currency. Reference has already been made to its great potential as a major safety value in relieving pressure on Community national currencies in the international exchange markets. However, its role as a parallel currency at domestic level within the Common Market could also be important. Once, for example, travellers' cheques circulate freely within the EEC and, most probably almost simultaneously, once more Member States allow their nationals to open banking accounts denominated in ECU's, then the road is open for the development of an important market in ECU's. The importance of the ECU would then lie in its attractiveness as an immediately available European currency - under European control - for Community nationals should their own governments embark upon the slippery path of unwise economic and monetary policies.

At this point, the road would be open for the development of open market operations in ECU's. This would, preferably, go hand-in-hand with the development of a "real" European Monetary Fund.

Most Recent official Proposals for the ECU.

In May 1983, the Commission made proposals [3] for the promotion of the private role of the ECU.

Although the full text of these proposals is reproduced in the appendices, the Commission does point out that ECU denominated issues make the unit of account the "most used currency, after the dollar and the DM, for the floating of bonds on the international markets". In view of this fact - and other considerations - the Commission calls for Community action concerning the status and the use of the ECU as well as the protection of the ECU trademark.

Final Observations

To the author, the overall view of the ECU and its future is very much that it is foredoomed to be successful. It embodies important qualities both as a currency as well as a reserve asset and its attraction as a "risk spreader" is particularly clear. Now, with its almost imminent introduction in use for travellers' cheques, its usage will become generalised - its use having hitherto been mainly restricted to official purposes. This implies that the restrictions to this unit of account by Community citizens - which have been bureaucratic and/or political - will disappear. However, this change means that the need for a greater Community control over the ECU markets will grow. In turn, this underlies the need for a real European Monetary Fund - or some similar central organ.

Chapter 7. The Convergence of National Economies.

Any future moves in the direction of the implementation of a full economic and monetary union will succeed or come to grief on the question of the convergence of the national economies. In the medium and long term, a failure to achieve convergence in the field of inflation rates, for example, could well lend to a repetition of the "Snake" experience with the EMS becoming divided between hard and weak currency areas. There are, therefore, three technical areas where action should be taken; these are, inflation rates, budgetary deficits and definitions of money supply.

In the very short run, differing rates of inflation are not, perhaps, as important as some economists might believe. This observation is based on two provisoes; these are, the bringing into play of a "portfolio" approach or a "near portfolio" approach towards the currency of a country suffering a high of inflation and/or balance-of-payments problems and/or high levels of public borrowing. In the former case, provided that foreigners (governments, banks, institutes and/or individuals) are prepared to hold the bonds and/or bills of the country whose currency is under pressure, then that currency may maintain an artificially high value for a relatively long period of time. Similarly, in the latter case, with the approach called by the author a "near-portfolio" one, so long as the afore-mentioned named foreigners are willing to hold the currency which is facing pressure on the exchange markets, then that currency may for a relatively long time, be able to ride out the storm. In the 1970's, both the U.S.Dollar and the Danish Krone, to mention only two currencies, were supported by the "portfolio" and "near-portfolio" attitudes of central banks and institutes - particularly by those of West Germany. However, in a de-facto monetary union or in a near-economic and monetary union, with the possible exception of perhaps one or two small economies, it is not possible for inflation rates to widen too greatly. The experience of the old "Snake" Arrangement provides sufficient support for this observation.

As has already been observed, during the first three years of the existence of the EMS (see: table No.3), inflation rates tended to rise and to widen between EEC Member States. Similarly, public borrowing and budget deficits tended to increase (see: table No.5). In both cases, the worst culprit was Italy. Also, the performance gap between that country and West Germany tended to widen. Although, in 1982 and 1983, the performance of some countries, particularly that of Belgium, the Netherlands, the United Kingdom and West Germany, tended to improve, the aforementioned gap remained.

There seems to be some connection between inflation rates and budget deficits. Caution should, however, be taken in examining this link since where a major part of public spending is on efficient, state owned industrial enterprises, the structure of such spending takes on a different complexion. Nevertheless, those countries which are adopting careful attitudes towards public spending are enjoying an improvement with inflation rates. Inevitably, public spending, especially when associated with budgetary deficits, has an effect on the monetary supply and on interest rates.

All these observations imply that the Member States of the EEC, whether they are participating in the EMS or not, would accelerate the moves towards the implementation of a full economic and monetary union if they were to make their inflation levels converge. One of the first steps in this direction would be to undertake a thorough examination of the public spending of the Member States. With or without such an examination the currencies of countries with a large public sector and with major budget deficits will continue to come under pressure and such countries will finally be placed before the choice of leaving the EMS, temporarily or definitively, or of putting their economic house in order.

The question of the definition of the money supply is rather a choice between a number of definitions than a question of one definition. This presents a problem because, as is indicated in Chapter 8 , EEC Member States tend not only to use different definitions, but even to drop one definition and then to choose another - sometimes over relatively short periods of time. Such a state of affairs will present problems should the EEC envisage an eventual move towards the implementation

TABLE No. 5

EEC : Member States : General Government Borrowing Requirements as a Percentage of GNP.

	1979	1980	1981
Belgium	7.0	9.4	13.1
Denmark	3.1	5.9	7.2
France	0.8	- 0.5	- 1.9
Germany (West)	3.0	3.5	4.5
Ireland	11.9	12.8	15.1
Italy	9.5	8.4	11.9
Netherlands	3.1	3.4	4.6
United Kingdom	3.3	2.5	2.4

Source: Eurostat and EEC Commission, "European Economy", No.12, July 1982 of a full EMU. A full EMU would inevitably imply a common monetary policy, probably managed by a central organ. A common monetary policy would normally imply a common definition of the monetary supply.

Technical Options for the EEC.

In the immediate future, the main technical problem for the Community is how to bring down inflation rates to similar low levels among the Member States. Reference has been made to the serious efforts being undertaken by some countries in an effort to achieve this goal - and to the fact that differences between some states remain. Reference has also been made to the technical considerations of budgetary deficits and the definition of the monetary supply. This latter question will be examined in greater depth in the following section.

Among all these considerations, the main problem is that of inflation. Here, it is possible (usually with the help of friendly central banks and similar institutions) for some (normally small) countries to ride out pressures for some time. However, as inflation rates continue to diverge, pressures for exchange rate adjustment increase.

To the author, the real technical option is to make it interesting for Member States to achieve low levels of inflation. To this end, the author has already proposed[4)] that "target" levels of inflation should be set for those Member States with high levels of inflation. Should these countries achieve these targets, the low inflation countries might consider transferring some resources to the former countries. In the meantime, studies should be undertaken concerning the role of budgetary deficits and the definition of money supply as causes of inflation. Here, also, once scientific evidence has been established about the role of these technical factors, target levels could also be set in both these fields.

Finally, if adequate convergence of economic and monetary policies among Member States does not materialise, the danger exists that the EMS will, like its predecessor, disintegrate into strong and weak monetary zones.

Chapter 8 : The Money Supply Question.

During the past decade, the question of the money supply in national economic policy management has assumed an importance of great magnitude. At the very base of such management is the definition of money supply. Some degree of concessus about this definition is important in an EMU. Basically, there are three definitions of money supply - these are set out below. However, as is shown in the remainder of this section, the Member States of the EEC do not use any common definition - this is perhaps a disturbing situation which will require further examination - should the Member States desire a greater degree of integration --- eventually leading to a full EMU.

The basic definitions of Money Supply are as follows:

M.1. : Currency in circulation
plus
Current (sight) Accounts with Commercial Banks and Similar institutes.

M.2. : Currency in circulation
plus
Current (sight) Accounts plus Deposit (Time) Accounts.
In principle, this definition implies funds borrowed for less than 4 years.

M.3. : M.2. plus Saving Accounts.

PSL.2 (United Kingdom): M.3 (Sterling) and building society deposits held by the private sector plus private sector holdings of other money market instruments (national savings securities, Treasury Bills, deposits with local authorities and finance houses) plus certificates of tax deposits.

France.

The French authorities use M.2. as the definition of money supply in their management of the national economy. They give the impression that they are satisfied with this definition. This has been made public since 1976.

West Germany.

Since 1974, the West German authorities have used a special interpretation of M.1. as their definition of money supply. This definition is the minimum reserve requirements at constant base plus currency in circulation.

United Kingdom.

The British authorities use a wide range of definitions of money supply in their management of national economic policy. Thus, three different aggregates are currently being used (since March 1982). These definitions are M.1, Sterling M.3 and PSL.2. Targets for the rate of growth of Sterling M.3 had been used since 1977.

Italy.

In Italy, a variation of the definition of M.2 money supply is used in national economic management. This definition is M.2 - being currency and notes plus bank deposits plus deposits with the General Post Office. This definition had been used since the 1950's. However, since 1976-77, when the State started selling large amounts of Treasury Bills to the public, the definition of M.2 has been enlarged to include Treasury Bills.

The Netherlands.

Since 1951, the Dutch authorities have used a special definition of M.2 of money supply in managing the country's economy. Clearly, they are satisfied with this definition which implies M.1 plus "Near Money", which excludes "genuine" savings. Quoting directly from the reply received from the Dutch Central Bank, their definition of "Near Money" represents "a liability of local authorities comprising money at call and temporary loans, and advances to provinces, municipalities and - insofar as recorded - to polder boards and joint boards, as well as claims of various description with an original maturity of less than two years on the Bank for Netherlands Municipalities and the Netherlands Polder Board Bank.

Near money representing a liability of banks and giro institutions, comprises claims with an original maturity of less than 2 years in the form of time deposits, foreign currency deposits and liquid savings deposits. Short-term time deposits also include call money and savings certificates to bearer of less than two years".

Denmark.

In simple terms, in Denmark, the money supply is defined as the private non-bank sector's liquid claims on the Government, the Danish Central Bank and the banking system. In reality, however, the Danes (like their British counterparts) use three different definitions. Thus, the narrow definition, the "Monetary Base" or B, implies claims on the Danish Central Bank and the Government, i.e., notes coin and deposits in Post Office Giro accounts.

The broader definition M.1, implies B plus demand deposits with banks. The broadest definition of M.2 implies M.1 plus holdings of Treasury Bills and time deposits with banks - but excluding certain tax privileged time deposits (such as deposits under pension schemes). The first two concepts have been used and published for decades. Until the beginning of 1982, the published M.2 was defined as M.1 plus all-time deposits with banks, i.e. excluding Treasury Bills and with no deduction for the afore-mentioned tax privileged time deposits.

Belgium.

The case of Belgium is perhaps the most special one in the EEC. In order to understand the author's observation on this point, the Belgian Central Bank's answer to the questionnaire is directly quoted: "The Belgian monetary authorities do not set intermediate quantitative targets in terms of 'money supply'. This is because the country is extremely open in terms of movements of goods and because incomes normally adjust themselves rapidly to prices and Belgium cannot afford to overlook its currency's external value. As in addition, capital movements are highly sensitive to the evolution of interest rate differentials, Belgium has to adjust its interest rate policy in the light of such capital movements. Belgium could not therefore set a quantitative monetary target without considering the implications for interest rates of the achievement of the target. It must retain a free hand in regard to interest rate policy".

Ireland.

For approximately the past ten years, the Irish definition of money supply has been extremely simple. The concept used is a broad one, M.3.

This definition includes accounts denominated in both Irish Pounds and foreign currency. However, the institutes covered are only licensed banks.

The Author's Observations

This overview of the definition of the money supply in different Community countries is perplexing. Some countries, such as France and the Netherlands, express satisfaction with the definition used over a number of years. In contrast, the United Kingdom, in a seemingly perpetual quest to include as many components as possible in the national monetary coverage, has tended, over time, to use the definition used, and, to have even coined a specifically British definition.

Only in one case, that of Belgium, is a clear reason given for the policy adopted, i.e. the non-pursuit of money supply objectives.

To the author, the real question, which only seems to have been partly considered in Britain, is the desirability of the amount of coverage in the definition. Thus, for example, should only money and "rear" money be included and should one exclude real savings? Perhaps the coverage should be wide because all bank deposits - whether in current (sight) or deposit (time) accounts - create lending ---- and consequently --- spending. Perhaps, in the field of monetary policy, it would be more wise to widen the coverage of institutes covered to include as many as possible. The author suspects that in some countries (especially in Ireland where only "licensed" banks are considered as being banks) a number of institutes are slipping through the monetary net. This would certainly be a useful study and research project to be undertaken by the Monetary Committee of the European Commission - or by some other body.

What is of real concern to the author is the fact that if and when the Community should wish to transform the EMS into an EMU, a common monetary management would certainly be one of the goals of such a union. But in order to have any degree of common monetary management some minimum common definition of monetary supply would be necessary. Some moves in this direction should preferably be undertaken in the near future.

NOTES : Part Three

1). Quoted from P.Coffey, "The Use of Reserve Asstes in the Framework of a European Economic and Monetary Union and World Monetary Reform", in "Système Monétaire Européen et Réforme Monétaire Mondiale", Editions de l'Université de Bruxelles, 1981.

2). The group of French banks comprises the Crédit Lyonnais, BNP, Caisse National de Crédit Agricole and the CCF.
(see: ECU Newsletter, no.5, May 1983, Turin, Italy).

3). Reference : COM (83) 274 Final - Brussels 24 May 1983.

4). See: P.Coffey, "Europe and Money", Macmillan, London, 1977.

PART FOUR : The Future of the EMS : The Integration of Capital Markets and Banking Systems.

Chapter 9 : A European Capital Market.

Writing some ten years ago[1], the author observed that the real European Capital Market was then the Euro-dollar market and that the centres for that market were London and Zürich - both at that time in countries not then belonging to the EEC. Apart from Britain's subsequent membership of the Common Market and a few other changes, including the growth of other important Euro-dollar centres, little seems to have changed since that time. Indeed, a recent communication from the Commission to the Council of Ministers[2] would seem to suggest that things have tended to go backwards. Instead of integrating their financial systems and using the now quite generous Community financial credits, they tend to have recourse to the use of the safeguard clauses (explained below) which allow them to re-introduce restrictions of one kind or another on capital movements.

Reasons and Preconditions for the integration of Capital Markets.

In any customs union - especially one such as the European Economic Community - the removal of the obstacles to the free movement of the factors of production, goods and services are fundamental principles. In the case of the Common Market, most of the aims as set down in the Treaty of Rome (establishing the customs union) were achieved by 1968. In the case of the freeing of capital movements, the Community, acting upon articles 67-73 (inclusive) of the Treaty of Rome, did enact a number of directives between 1960 and 1963[3], which, in principle, at least freed capital movements between EEC Member States. Thus, the stage was set for the creation of a European Capital Market.

Segré, writing in his famous report in 1964[4], listed four main reasons why the Community should develop just such a capital market. He felt that such a development would:

(i) lead to an increase in savings,

(ii) reduce distortions in competition,

(iii) lead to an optimum utilisation of funds, and

(iv) help to regulate aggregate money demand through the speeding-up of necessary counter-cyclical policy.

The author, whilst querying the realism of the fourth of Segré's expectations - mainly because of the use of different policy instruments by the different Community Member States, does support the first three points. Regarding competition, nowhere, it seems is the broom of real competition needed more than in the banking and financial fields. Indeed, the author has always been surprised that the effective Competition Directorate of the Commission has not used articles 85 and 86 of the Treaty of Rome in these fields. Any move whatsoever that gives the citizens of the Community access to more information about and makes more transparent the fiscal and banking markets is to be welcomed.

To the expectations listed by Segré, the author would list his own reasons why the Community should develop a European Capital Market. Thus, such a development would:

(i) lead to a greater degree of 'transparency' in the supply of funds and therefore improve efficiency,

(ii) probably help regional needs because it is likely that some Member States would insist on the creation of real Community regional plans, more generous regional funds and even Community regional investment banks as a precondition for accepting the integration of capital markets,

(iii) encourage specialisation in certain centres through the greater use of existing services and traditions,

(iv) increase the Community's control over EEC borrowing on the capital markets,

(v) possibly diminish the necessity of EEC borrowing on non-Community markets, and,

(vi) facilitate the use and movement of balance-of-payments surpluses between creditor and deficit countries in the Common Market.

Particular EEC Conditions and the Capital Markets.

Although, as has just been outlined, the main preconditions for the integration of capital markets are quite clear, there also exist conditions - particular to the EEC - which deserve careful consideration. Among these, the most important ones are:

(i) the size of the national debt in EEC Member States and the dates of its maturity,

(ii) the degree of influence by the national authorities over the bond markets, and

(iii) the degree of priority given by national capital markets to domestic and public sector borrowers.

The question of national debt is important because in any future real moves in integrating capital markets, the responsibility for shouldering national debt will have to be faced. Similarly, heavy borrowing by public authorities in some countries will increase competition for credit in the markets.

Intervention by public authorities to influence the bond markets also restricts competition - as does the giving of priority to domestic borrowers. This latter situation would be quite unacceptable in an integrated capital market, since it could result in the exclusion of other Community borrowers from individual national capital markets.

Basically, all these considerations are governed by the fundamental questions of competition and an optimal allocation of resources. Similarly, the degree of freedom of access to all EEC capital markets by Community citizens and enterprises will depend on the adoption of clear policies towards these considerations. However, even if all such considerations are properly examined and any necessary measures adopted, the most important problem then remaining in integrating capital markets would be the granting by Member States to their citizens and enterprises of the right to freely borrow on the capital markets of other Community countries. At the time of writing, among EEC States, only the United Kingdom allows capital to move without hindrance in and out of the country.

Government Influence on the Capital Markets.

When considering the degree of integration existing at the present time in the capital markets of the European Economic Community, it is necessary to attempt to calculate the degree to which governments influence these markets. Thus, the author has put the following five questions to the central banks of Common Market countries, asking whether the government (in each country) influences the stock exchange through:

(i) official intervention in the bond market?

(ii) through intervention to stabilise short-term bond prices?

(iii) through influence over the slope and position of the yield curve?

(iv) through the giving of priority to public sector borrowing?

(v) through the giving of priority to domestic borrowing?

The answers to these questions indicate that, outside the community legislation, there has been some convergence in government policy towards capital markets in the different countries. This development is also duplicated by a growing similarity in banking services now being offered in most states in the Common Market.

In the field of capital market integration, the case of each country is therefore examined individually.

France.

(i) In France there is no direct State intervention on the bond markets - but influence is exercised by such para-State institutions as the Caisse des Dépots.

(ii) Intervention on short-term bond prices is made through the taxation system.

(iii) The government makes no direct influence as such on the slope and position of the yield curve - but the structure of interest rates is an influence in encouraging saving.

(iv) Both the Treasury and the Comité des Émissions influence the priority given to public sector borrowing.

(v) In France, there is, as such, little foreign borrowing - therefore it is difficult to speak of priority being given to domestic borrowers.

Despite the understandably non-commital replies made by the Banque de France, an impression is nevertheless gained that the State does ensure that some degree of priority is given both to domestic as well as (and especially) to State enterprises. However, at a structural level, the mitigating factor is that the capital markets (meaning recourse to the stock exchange) are not so well developed in France as in some countries. In contrast, industry, both private and state, makes considerable use of banking finance. Here, it is possible to discern the giving of a degree of priority to State enterprises. This trend is likely to expand as a result of the nationalisation of banks and commercial enterprises under the Mitterand Government.

West Germany.

(i) In West Germany, there is limited intervention by authorities in the bond market. This intervention is undertaken in order to maintain an orderly market.

(ii) In contrast with (i), the authorities do not intervene to stabilise short-term bond prices.

(iii) Similarly, the authorities exercise no influence on the slope and position of the yield curve.

(iv) In contrast with some countries, in West Germany, no priority is given to the public sector borrowing.

(v) Until 1979, the level of domestic public sector borrowing was low. Since that date, however, domestic borrowing has increased. It is nevertheless difficult to speak of the giving of priority to domestic borrowing. To the author, the present situation might lead to a limited "crowding out" of foreign borrowers by domestic ones.

The answers given by the Bundesbank indicate, as was expected, that intervention by the authorities in West Germany is, for all intents and purposes, quite negligible. Indeed, in comparison with France, one could say that the West German capital market is completely free and competitive for all practical purposes.

United Kingdom.

The British capital market, centred on the City of London, is the most important one in Europe and one of the two main centres in the world. The London capital market functions at three levels: the domestic, the international (sterling) and the Euro-currency/dollar levels. In this study, we are concerned with the first two.

When considering the British domestic capital market it is important to bear in mind that the British Government and local (municipal) authorities have enormous recourse to the stock exchange. In fact, a situation exists whereby the long-term bond market is dominated to a degree of 100 per cent (on occasions, even more than 100 per cent!) by the State. Therefore, it is reasonable to talk of a "crowding out" effect by the Government in the long-term bond market. This fact has been taken into account when analysing the replies given by the Bank of England.

(i) The aim of the British authorities is to maximise the long-term desire of investors at home and abroad to hold British Government Debt. To the author, this implies some degree of intervention by the authorities in order to make such bonds attractive.

(ii) Since 1971, intervention by the authorities in the short-term market has been limited.

(iii) Intervention here takes the form of promoting and sustaining the most appropriate pattern of interest rates and through limiting government borrowing from the banking system.

(iv) (v) Here, priority is not overtly given to the public sector and to domestic borrowing.

Although the British Authorities do not "overtly" interven in the capital markets - and this is certainly the case in the short-term markets since 1971 - the very fact that the State almost completely dominates the long-term domestic capital market means that there is little or nothing left over for anyone else. Furthermore, since official policy has more recently attempted to reduce Government recourse to the banking system, logically State recourse to the stock exchang is increased still further. Whilst State intervention is not so overt as in France, the needs of the British Government are such that the end effect in the long-term market is much greater than is the case in France.

Italy.

(i) The authorities in Italy do occasionally intervene in the bond markets.

(ii) Similarly, intervention is made in the short-term bond market.

(iii) The authorities do influence the slope and position of the yield curve.

(iv) Overtly, priority is not given to public sector borrowing. However, the needs of this sector have, in recent years, tended to increase and the attractiveness of State debt lead to a "crowding out" effect regarding other borrowers.

(v) The situation described in (iv) and the exchange controls lead to a situation where domestic borrowing occupies a most important position.

The situation in Italy shows that the authorities do officially intervene in the capital markets. Also, the very important public sector in that country - together with the increasingly important public debt - imply that there is a "crowding out" effect in these markets. The situation appears to be somewhat similar to that existing in the United Kingdom.

The Netherlands.

As in other Common Market countries, responsibility for the supervision of the capital markets in the Netherlands lies with the central bank. Also, as is the case in Western Germany, this responsibility really takes the form of "preserving orderly market conditions" in the primary bond markets through the simple use of an issue calendar.

(i) Despite the afore-mentioned reference to the supervising role of the central bank, it is the Ministry of Finance which intervenes occasionally in the secondary bond market to "preserve a good market climate" - especially, apparently, when issuing a new bond loan.

(ii) The authorities do not intervene to stabilise short-term bond prices.

(iii) Equally, influence over the slope and position of the yield curve is not exercised.

(iv) Priority is given to public sector borrowing.

(v) Although, as in the case of West Germany, it is difficult to observe the giving of priority to domestic borrowing, the recent increases in State borrowing would tend to lead to a degree of "crowding out" of other borrowers, similar to the situation being observed in other EEC countries.

At first sight, the situation existing in the Dutch capital markets would seem to be more similar to the West German position than to that found in other countries. However, regarding point (iv) and the priority given to public/State borrowing, the situation is obviously quite different and would appear to be much more like the situation existing in Belgium and France.

Denmark.

As in a number of Common Market countries, the role of the Danish Central Bank in the capital markets is to maintain an orderly situation and to make government loans attractive to prospective creditors. However, the major government budgetary deficits in Denmark certainly colour the climate in the capital markets and must make some degree of intervention necessary. Thus, the answers shown below have been heavily interpreted by the author.

(i) The central bank intervenes in the bond market to make government loans attractive.

(ii) There appears to be little intervention to stabilise short-term bond prices.

(iii) There appears to be some influence exercised over the slope and position of the yield curve.

(iv) Although it is difficult to conclude that priority is given to public sector borrowing, the recent heavy demands of the public sector must lead to a "crowding out" of other borrowers.

(v) Overtly, priority does not appear to be given to domestic borrowing. However, as in (iv) the heavy State demands must in effect, lead to the giving of some degree of priority to domestic borrowers.

The situation in Denmark would, at first sight, to be rather nebulous ----- with the central bank attempting, as in the United Kingdom, to make government loans attractive to creditors. In reality, however, the recent heavy financial needs of the State must have lead to a degree of "crowding out" of private and foreign borrowers.

Ireland.

In Ireland, two major considerations dominate the role played by the authorities in the capital markets. On the one hand, as a result of the "comparative thinness" for Government paper in the country, it is necessary for the authorities to be active in the bond market to make State loans attractive. On the other hand, the recent heavy budget deficits and the necessity to having incrased recourse to domestic rather than foreign sources of finance have placed great pressures on the capital markets. Thus, the former situation whereby the authorities attempt to increase the attractiveness of Government paper has been reinforced by the second development ---- the seemingly almost insatiable State demands for finance.

(1) The authorities intervene in the bond market to increase the attractiveness of Government paper. The Ministry of Finance intervenes in the long-term market.

(ii) The Central Bank intervenes to stabilise short-term bond prices.

(iii) The authorities attempt to influence the slope and the position of the yield curve.

(iv) Although overt priority does not appear to be given to the public sector borrowing, the great financial demands of the State tend to lead to a "crowding out" of other borrowers.

(iv) The situation described in (iv) and the former heavy borrowing by the Irish Government abroad imply that there would be no or little place for foreign borrowers on the Irish Capital Market.

Belgium and Luxembourg.

Since 1921, a monetary union has existed between Belgium and Luxembourg. In this union, it is Belgium which is mainly responsible for monetary affairs. Therefore, unless otherwise stated, the expression Belgium is also intended to include Luxembourg.
In Belgium, rather than in Luxembourg, in recent years, a most important budget deficit has persistently been recorded. Although, as in France and Italy, the State has traditionally had a major recourse to banking finance (as compared for example with the United Kingdom and the Netherlands), the constant budget deficits have forced the State to have increased recourse to the stock exchange. This fact clearly colours the author's interpretation of the answers to the questionnaire.

(i) In Belgium, "the Securities Regulation Fund, an official institution does intervene in the bond market to avoid erratic fluctuations in the prices of Government bonds". *)

(ii) The Treasury does intervene - through the planning of the launching of loans to stabilise short-term bond prices.

(iii) The Treasury does influence the scope and position of the yield curve.

(iv) Although there is no evidence to suggest the giving of priority to public sector borrowing, the fact that the Treasury is the main borrower in the capital market, there is, as in some other Common Market countries, a "crowding out" of other borrowers.

(v) Priority is not given to domestic borrowing.

In Luxembourg, the LMI (Luxembourg Monetary Instituut - see: note on page 139) possesses the power both to regulate domestic credit and to intervene in the capital markets and the foreign exchange market (this power is not normally used). However, in the case of the market for public issues, an official calendar is established by the LMI - and priority is given to public sector borrowing. In the case of private bond issues, whilst no official calendar exists, priority has to be given to candidates using funds collected in Luxembourg or Belgium.

*) Quoted directly from the Central Bank Answers to the questionnaire.

Further Observations.

The current situation (summer/autumn 1983), observed in the Community's capital markets, is indeed a mixed one. With the exception of West Germany, in all countries there is evidence of State intervention. Even where intervention does not directly take place, the sometimes very heavy government appetites for funds tends to lead to a state of "crowding out" for other borrowers. All this implies that there remains much work to be done in improving competition and access by all Community nationals and enterprises to all Community capital markets before the EMS could reach a more advanced stage of integration - perhaps then leading to an EMU. But, if this is to be achieved one area where action would have to be taken would be in the field of national debt in the individual Member States.

The National Debt.

The persistent and large budget deficits being experienced in recent years in a number of countries clearly underlines the importance of the national debt. Here, there are a number of important considerations - among which the most important are:

(i) the actual size of the debt as a percentage of the gross national product (GNP),

(ii) the maturity of the debt, and,

(iii) the tendency for the budget deficits to increase or to decrease.

France.

In 1980, the French national debt stood at 10.2 per cent of the G.N.P. The general trend is to shorten the length (the maturity) of the debt - with a normal maximum being 15 years. In 1980, for example, the three State loans made were for 10, 6 and 7 years, respectively.

At the end of 1983, the precise structure of the maturity of the national debt was:

under 2 years	:	64.7 per cent of total
2 to 4 years	:	8.0 " " " "
4 to 6 years	:	16.0 " " " "
6 to 8 years	:	9.0 " " " "
8 to 10 years	:	1.0 " " " "
10 to 12 years	:	1.0 " " " "

more than 12 years : 1.0 per cent of total.

In France, the most recent trend is for the State to reduce the budget deficit.

West Germany

In 1982, the West German national debt amounted to 19.2 per cent of the GNP. The majority of the debt is of a short term nature - although a surprisingly large percentage is of long maturity:

	as percentage of total:
less than 4 years :	28.8
4 to 10 years :	44.5
more than 10 years:	26.7

The most recent tendency in West Germany is for the Government to reduce spending.

United Kingdom.

Although Government spending in Britain is among the lowest in the Common Market, the national debt is large; in 1981/2 it stood at 42.6 per cent of the GNP. Also, a large percentage of the debt is of long-dated maturity:

	on 31 March 1982	on 31 March 1983
	as percentage of total	
Marketable Debt		
0 to 5 years	21.0	22.0
0 to 15 years	29.0	28.0
over 15 years	24.0	23.0
Undated	3.0	2.0
Non-Marketable Debt		
less than 3 months	5.0	5.0
3 months to 5 years	16.0	19.0
over 5 years	2.0	1.0

The tendency of the British Government is to reduce State-spending.

Italy.

The Italian national debt is tending to increase. Thus, at the end of 1982, the total stood at 330,223 billion Lire. A year later, in September 1983, this sum had increased to 392,950 billion Lire.

In contrast with the size of this debt, the maturity dates tend to be relatively short. The average maturity is 15 months - 27 months for medium - and long-term debt and only 5 months for Treasury bills.

Although the increasing size of Italy's national debt causes concern, its short-term nature reduces the fundamental problem that may be encountered in a full economic and monetary union. The situation in Italy is in particularly strong contrast with that of Britain.

The Netherlands.

At the end of 1982, the total of the net national debt*) of the Netherlands stood at 138,321 millions of guilders. The major part of this debt was short - or medium - term in structure. The precise structure of the Dutch national debt was as follows:

Maturity:		As a Percentage of Total:
less than 5 years	:	40
between 5 and 10 years	:	40
between 10 and 15 years	:	12
between 15 and 20 years	:	3
between 20 and 25 years	:	1
over 25 years	:	4

Denmark.

Denmark is currently running a government deficit equal to about 12 per cent of the GNP. This deficit has tended to increase persistently since 1976. Major increases were noted in the years 1979, 1980 and 1981. The outcome is that the total national debt at the end of December 1982 amounted to 204 billion Krone or 44 per cent of the GNP. In this respect, the Danish position is very similar to that of the United Kingdom.

Whilst the total Danish debt has tended to increase, the foreign currency debt has also increased quite dramatically.

*) this excludes debts incurred by local authorities.

Traditionally, the mass of Danish national debt was of a very short-term nature with a maturity of between 1 and 2 years. Since 1.April, 1981, however, issues of 1 year bills were suspended in an attempt to increase the maturity of government debt. Also, during the period 1975 to 1978 , government bond issues were of either long-term or, more especially, medium-term (3 to 12 years maturity). Then, in the autumn of 1980, unusually for Denmark, a government bond issue with a maturity of 20 years was made.

Ireland.

On 31. December, 1982, the total Irish National Debt stood at £.12,816.7 million. The structure of this debt was as follows:

Maturity:		As a Percentage of Total:
between 0 and 5 years	:	30.9
between 5 and 10 years	:	14.6
between 10 and 15 years	:	6.9
between 15 and 20 years	:	9.4
over 20 years	:	15.8
not allocated	:	22.4

These figures indicate that whilst a substantial amount of the debt is of a relatively short-term nature, the majority (as in the case of the United Kingdom) is either medium - or long - term. Thus, like Britain, Ireland would face some problems should the present EMS be transformed into a fully fledged EMU.

Belgium.

At the end of 1983, the total Belgian National Debt stood at 3,716 billion francs. Of this, 824 billions were in foreign currencies.

Most of this debt is of a short - or medium - term nature. There is very little, if any with a maturity of over twenty years. This situation implies that Belgium would not face undue problems in a full EMU on considerations of the maturity of the national debt. However, as in the case of Denmark, the existence of large amounts of foreign currencies as a major component would be likely to present certain problems for the union.

Luxembourg.

At the end of 1983, the total public debt of Luxembourg amounted to just over 40 billion Francs (the structure of this debt may be found on page 66).

The Author's Observations.

According to the 1983 communication on Financial Integration (see: Appendix IV), sent by the Commission to the Council, the freeing of the intra-Community capital movements is now less free than it was in the 1960's. To the author, for all intents and purposes, the EEC had, by 1968, achieved freedom of capital movements. Thereafter, following the monetary upheavals and exchange rate adjustments of 1969, countries have tended to use the escape clause embodied in the relevant directives of the early 1960's in order to control capital movements. As the Commission stressed in its communication, Member State Governments have nearly always tended not to use Community credits which are intended to help countries facing balance-of-payments and similar problems. The exception to this situation has been the recourse, by France, in 1983, to a massive Community "jumbo" loan - using the co-called Ortoli Facility. Unfortunately, at the time of writing (May, 1984), only half of the Member States (the Benelux countries, the United Kingdom and West Germany) do not impose restrictions on capital movements.

Despite this somewhat sombre picture, the author is now somewhat more optimistic about the future for capital movement liberalisation in the EEC. Capital movements will only be freed - together with some subsequent degree of capital market integration - when currency stability exists between Community countries. The EMS is in the process of achieving this. For the first time in two decades, all, except one of the EEC Member States, have adopted the same public economic policy choice - namely, the control of inflation. Inflation rates have, over the past year, been falling, and, what is more important, they are, in some cases, tending to converge. Furthermore, the draconian economic measures being taken by countries such as Belgium and France - together with a beginning of a change in national economic management in Italy - all augure well for the future. Should the present trends continue, then it should be possible for most Community countries to free capital movements.

In order to be ready to benefit more fully from such a

liberalisation, it would be wise if Member States, were, in advance, to implement some of the Commission's proposals (as contained in Appendix IV) for linking up national stock exchanges (bourses) as well as other organisational measures.

Some of the policy measures adopted in the control of inflation include a reduction in the budget deficits of the Member States. Such moves are important not only in reducing levels of inflation - but also in the context of the national debt which is a most important factor which must be taken into account should the Community wish to transform the present EMS into a full EMU. The situation described in this chapter does, in the case of some countries, give cause for concern. This is particularly so, for example, where in countries such as Denmark and the United Kingdom, not only does the national debt constitute an important percentage of the GNP, but a substantial part of this debt tends to be long-term in character. In a fully integrated European Capital Market, the question of the assumption of responsibility for these debts by the Community would certainly have to be tackled. Similarly, any excessive recourse by the State to the capital markets would tend to "crowd out" other borrowers. These are all long-term considerations which nevertheless deserve deep study, preferably in the near future, by the Commission and/or other similar bodies.

In conclusion, then, it is clear that no progress has been made in liberalising capital movements between Community Member States since the 1960's. Countries, when facing balance-of-payments and similar problems have nearly always used the escape clause of the relevant directives in order to restrict capital movements. Thus, an integrated European Capital Market would now seem to be further away than was the case in the 1960's.

At the structural level, nearly all Governments of the EEC Member States influence the capital markets (bourses) in some way or other. Some tend to give priority to domestic lending. Others, whilst not doing so specifically, use up so many of the financial resources available, that, in effect, there is little if anything, left for foreign borrowers. In some way or other (either directly or through public institutes) all States use their influence to maintain a degree of order on the stock exchanges.

Clearly, in an integrated capital market, Governments would have to relinquish their excessive priviliged access to the capital markets - except by offering attractive financial inducements to lenders. Certainly, administrative obstacles to the entry of other Community borrowers on national capital markets would have to cease. However, concerning an orderly management of the capital markets - which is a necessary prerequisite for the smooth functioning of such institutions - national bodies could be replaced by a Community Capital Issues Committee - as the author suggested several years ago.

Finally, in the immediate future, the author is optimistic because nearly all Member States now appear to be serious in their determination to control inflation. This implies that (as has been the case since March 1983) a degree of currency stability inside the EEC should now be feasible. In turn, countries will have fewer, if any, excuses for maintaining controls over capital movements. The next step could be the beginning of the creation of a European Capital Market.

Footnote

The structure of the national debt in Luxembourg is as follows:

Maturity		as a percentage of Total
Under 5 years	:	21
Under ten years	:	65
Between 10 and 20 years	:	14

In Luxembourg, the tendency is for the periods of maturity to become shorter. The longest period of maturity was formerly 50 years - whereas the latest ones have a life of 8 years.

Chapter 10. A European Banking System.

An integrated European banking system is the obvious complement to a European capital market. This complementarity is based on the heavy reliance by industry and other parts of the economy on capital market financing in some countries (e.g. the Netherlands and the United Kingdom) and on banking financing in others (e.g. Italy and West Germany).

Basically speaking, there are three main reasons why an integrated banking system is desirable in a customs union such as the EEC. These are:

(i) the existence of a fundamental need for a great improvement in competition and in the provision of services ---- thereby increasing the welfare of Common Market citizens,

(ii) the necessity of reducing the claustrophobic role of banking syndicates and cartels within the EEC, and

(iii) the overall desirability of a better allocation of resources.

The situation in the field of banking in the Community is still most diverse, and, the author is forced to observe that practically no progress at all has been made in integrating this sector. As in the area of capital market integration, the author is surprised that the Commission has not made use of articles 85 and 86 of the Treaty of Rome in controlling concentration in the banking sector.

At this point, it is necessary to examine the structural situation in banking in the EEC. Referring to diagram No. 4 and Appendix VI , major differences between countries may be observed. At the top of the structure in each country the central bank has a different degree of responsibility for national economic and monetary management. At one extreme, the Bundesbank (the West German Central Bank) enjoys a high degree of independence. In fact, according to the West German Constitution the Bundesbank is endowed with responsibility for managing monetary policy and controlling inflation. Not endowed with the same degree of independence, the Bank of Italy does nevertheless enjoy a major supervisory role in the economic and monetary sphere. Also, because of the professional excellence of the directors of Italy's central bank and that country's

DIAGRAM No.4.

The European Economic Community - The Banking Systems: Summer 1983.

Country:	Degree of state ownership Central Bank	Main Commercial Banks (deposit)	Possibility of ownership by commercial banks of shares in industrial/commercial companies
Belgium	Fifty p.cent	No	Yes - through holding companies - but carefully restricted.
Denmark	complete	No	Yes - shares only - but limits are imposed on percentage of Bank's Funds used for these purposes.
France	complete	Yes	Yes, normally through holding companies.
Ireland	complete	No	Yes, but within certain specific limits.
Italy	yes- by publ. and semi-publ. instit. & comm.banks	Yes	Not normally allowed to own shares.
Luxembourg	Yes - (National Savings Bank)	No	Yes.
Netherlands	Yes	Government has a stake in some and a 33.33% stake in NMB	Yes - but only up to a maximum of 5%.
West Germany	Yes	No	Yes - without restriction.
United Kingdom	Yes	No	Yes - but not traditionally done.

recurrent political crisis, the Bank of Italy's importance and relative independence have tended to increase.

At the other end of the spectrum, the Banque de France is controlled by the French government. This control is reinforced by the State's management of monetary policy through the National Credit Council. Other central banks in the Community tend to fall somewhere between these two extremes regarding the degree of responsibility and independence which they enjoy in the management of national economic and monetary policy.

Whilst an equalisation of powers enjoyed by central banks has never been raised as one of the aims of an economic and monetary integration and/or an integration of capital markets and/or banking systems, the differing degree of powers given to central banks will have a most important influence on any future transformation of the EFMC into a "real" Fund.

The really important factors of concern in an EMU are:

(i) the obligation of commercial banks to give priority in their lending facilities to the public sector *),

(ii) the freedom of the main commercial banks to own shares in commercial and industrial enterprises and holding companies,

(iii) the freedom of commercial banks to offer diverse banking and auxiliary services to customers,

(iv) the degree of monopoly power enjoyed by banks and/or cartels in individual Member States and in the Community as a whole, and

(v) the possibility of individual banks based in one EEC country to open branches in other Member States.

*) *linked with this factor is the degree of ownership of the main commercial banks by the state.*

Special National Characteristics of the Banking Sector.

When examining capital market integration, it is necessary to ascertain the degree of competition existing in the banking sector as well as in the capital market (stock exchanges or bourses) proper. Thus, as in the case of the stock exchanges, the author sent a supplementary questionnaire about banking to the central banks of the Common Market countries. The precise aims of this questionnaire were to ascertain to what degree, if any, the public authorities encourage or put pressure on commercial banks to give priority to domestic borrowers, public and private. Similarly, it was hoped to be able to determine the degree of competition existing in the banking sector in the EEC. Also, the degree of State ownership of commercial banks is important and it is useful to be able to judge just how much these banks are themselves (through ownership, for example) linked with business enterprises. Thus, in this questionnaire, the author asked the following four precise questions:

1. To what degree are commercial banks in your country obliged to give priority in their lending facilities to the public sector?
2. To what degree may commercial banks in your country own shares in commercial and industrial enterprises or in holding companies?
3. Are commercial banks in your country allowed to offer diverse banking and ancillary services to clients?
4. To what degree are private financial institutions in your country expected to channel part of their funds through State agencies?

As was to be expected, in some countries - more than in others - the State does indeed influence bank lending. Then, the degree to which banks may own commercial enterprises also differs from country to country. However, the commercial banks in Common Market countries, have, over the past twenty years, tended to move in the same direction in that they have tried to emulate the West German banks in offering a more diverse choice of services to their customers. Nevertheless, as the following individual country studies show, there is much room for an improvement in competition in banking in the Community. Progress in this field will be one of the pre-conditions for the successful achievement of a full economic and monetary union.

France.

In France, the following situation may be observed:

1. A certain degree of self-limitation on bank lending is imposed on the commercial banks. Equally, these banks are encouraged to give some degree of priority in their lending to the public sector.

2. In principle, commercial banks may own shares in business enterprises. However, as in the United Kingdom, this is not done very much. Normally, such a practice is exercised through financial holding companies or groups - which are now nationalised.

3. Since 1966, commercial banks have been allowed to go into non-traditional forms of activities - thus offering a more diverse choice of services to their customers. In practice, ancillary services are offered by sub-branches of banks.

4. Private financial institutions are normally obliged to subscribe a certain amount of their finances to the public sector. This is generally done through specialised State agencies.

France, then, gives the impression of being a country where the State exercises some degree of pressure over the direction of bank lending. Since the massive nationalisations of banks undertaken by the Mitterand Government, it is fair to conclude that this control is likely to increase in future years.

West Germany.

In West Germany, the commercial banks find themselves in a totally different position from their French counterparts. The answers received to the author's questionnaire clearly indicate that the West German banks enjoy a degree of freedom which is rarely to be found in other Common Market countries.

(i) The commercial banks are under no obligation to give priority in their lending facilities to the public sector.

(ii) There is no limit on the freedom of commercial banks to own shares in commercial and industrial enterprises or on holding companies. In reality, however, these holdings are much less important than is commonly supposed.

(iii) Commercial banks in West Germany have long been the precursors in the diverse variety of services they may offer to their clients.

(iv) There is no obligation on commercial banks to channel any part of their funds through State agencies.

The banking situation in West Germany is clearly one of free enterprise with the banks linked particularly closely with commerce and industry. There are also no obligations on the banks to channel any of their funds in the direction of the State.

The United Kingdom.

In the United Kingdom, the tremendous recourse by the Government to the stock exchange diminishes Staterecourse to the banking sector. This therefore makes the British banking system more similar to the West German one rather than the French System.

(i) Commercial banks are not obliged to give priority to lending to the public sector.

(ii) There is no limit to banks holding shares in companies - but prudence is normally exercised in this matter. In practice, British commercial banks lend to industrial enterprises but do not own shares in them.

(iii)British commercial banks have, in recent years, been allowed to diversify the types of services they may offer to their customers.

(iv) There is no obligation on private financial institutions to channel any part of their funds through State agencies.

In principle, the commercial banking situation in Britain would appear to be very similar to the one existing in West Germany. This is particularly so regarding the lack of any obligation on commercial banks to give priority in their lending to the public sector or to channel part of their funds through State agancies.

At the more commercial level, although British banks may own shares in industrial enterprises - they rarely do so. Equally, although commercial banks may offer a wider range of services to their customers than was formerly the case, they still do not offer the same extent of services as those offered by their West German counterparts.

Italy.

In Italy, co-operation rather than coercion, between the State and the commercial banking system seems to be the order of the day. However, concerning the areas of banking activities, it is important to note that the banking law of 1936 has rigidly defined these. Further, commercial banking in Italy tends to be regionalised rather than centralised.

(i) In Italy, commercial banks are under no obligation to give priority in their lending to the public sector. However, "some degree of co-operation" between the two sides is customary.

(ii) There is practically no ownership by commercial banks of shares in commercial and industrial enterprises. This state of affairs results from the banking law of 1936 which separated commefcial from investment banking.

(iii) Commercial banks are allowed to offer diverse services to their customers through affiliates. In this manner, through the latter they may engage in operations in leasing, factoring and other financial services.

(iv) Commercial banks in Italy are not under any obligation to channel part of their funds through State agencies. However, in practice, because of the lack of risk associated with them and the attractive remuneration offered, commercial banks normally channel some of their funds through these agencies.

Thus, the situation in Italy differs from that found in the three EEC countries already examined. Co-operation between the commercial banks and the State clearly exists. However, commercial banks are much more restricted in their freedom to own shares in commercial and industrial enterprises. Also, whilst commercial banks may engage in other activities through afiliates, the situation is very different from that found in West Germany where the banks may directly offer many varied services to customers.

The Netherlands.

The Dutch commercial banking system would seem to be the one which is closest in type to the West German one. Like the latter model, the commercial banks find themselves under no obligation to lend to the State. However, unlike their German counterparts, the Dutch commercial banks are under carefully defined and strict limitations regarding the possibility of owning shares in commercial and industrial enterprises.

(i) In the Netherlands the commercial banks are under no obligation to give priority in their lending activities to the public sector.

(ii) Credit institutions are NOT allowed (unless prior approval is obtained) to hold more than 5 per cent in other enterprises or institutions.

(iii) Commercial banks are allowed to offer diversified services to their customers.

(iv) Private financial institutions are not expected to channel any part of their funds to State agencies.

Thus, the Dutch and West German commercial banking systems would appear to enjoy a similar degree of freedom in their activities. Certainly, in the large variety of services which they offer to customers the Dutch banks seem to be the closest to the West Germans among Common Market countries. Nevertheless, in the limitations on their freedom to hold shares in commercial and industrial enterprises they seem to be closer to their Italian than their German counterparts.

Denmark.

The Danish commercial banking system would seem to be even closer to the West German model than is the case with the Dutch system. As in both West Germany and the Netherlands, Danish commercial banks are under no obligation to channel part of their funds to the State. Like the West Germans, they may own shares in commercial and industrial enterprises. Although certain limits on this freedom are placed on the banks they are less rigid than in the Netherlands. As in West Germany, Danish commercial banks may offer different services to their customers.

(i) "The commercial banks and the savings banks in Denmark are not obliged to give priority in their lending facilities to the public sector." *)

(ii) According to the "Commercial Banks and Saving Banks Act , banks are forbidden to own - or grant loans on - shares in any one joint stock company or institution to an amount which exceeds fifteen per cent of the bank's own funds. The total value of the shares acquired by a bank may not exceed fifty per cent of the bank's own funds. Likewise, banks are forbidden to acquire shares in a commercial bank or

guarantee certificates in a savings bank to an amount exceeding thirty per cent of the share capital of a commercial bank or the guarantee capital of a savings bank. In general, it is laid down in the said act that commercial banks and savings banks shall not engage in any other activities than banking business.
Consequently, any acquisition of shares by banks has to be a portfolio investment." ✱

(iii) In Denmark, both commercial banks and the savings banks may offer many different services to their customers. However, it is not possible for Danish residents to own or undertake operations in gold bullion.

(iv) No form of obligation whatever is placed on private financial institutions to channel any part of their funds through State agencies.

In Denmark, then, the commercial banks clearly enjoy considerable freedom. They would seem to be very close to their West German counterparts. Although there exist clearly defined and precise limits on their participation in commercial and industrial enterprises, these are nevertheless less rigid than those imposed on their Dutch counterparts.

Ireland.

The obligations imposed on commercial banks in the Republic of Ireland concerning lending to the State are of a very basic kind - linked, in effect, to the secondary liquidity ratio which they are required to maintain. As in a number of EEC countries, licenced banks may own shares in commercial and industrial enterprises - but careful limits are imposed on this freedom. Also, as in a number of other Common Market countries, these banks may offer a wide variety of services to their customers.

(i) All commercial banks are required to maintain a secondary liquidity ration which is held mainly in the form of quoted Gevernment paper (both Exchequer Bills and Government bonds). Apart from this basic requirement, commercial banks are not required to give priority in their lending to the public sector.

(ii) "Licensed banks may own shares in commercial and industrial

✱) These parts are quoted directly from the Danish Central Bank's replies.

enterprises and in holding companies. However, such share holdings in another company may not exceed 20 per cent of the voting shares of that company without the written consent of the Central Bank. Moreover, not more than 2 per cent of a bank's total risk assets (the sum of loans and investments) may be employed with any one non-financial business in which it has what is considered by the Central Bank to be a major interest" ✱)

(iii) In Ireland, licensed banks are allowed to offer a wide variety of services to their customers.

(iv) Outside the secondary liquidity ration (described in (i)) licensed banks, other private domestic financial institutions in the Irish Republic are under no obligation to channel any part of their funds through State agencies.

As in a number of Common Market countries the commercial banks in the Republic of Ireland appear to enjoy a large amount of freedom in their activities. Although there are clear limits on their ownership of shares in commercial and industrial enterprises, these would not appear to be somewhat less rigid than those imposed on their Dutch counterparts.

Belgium and Luxembourg.

In the previous chapter on a "European Capital Market", reference was made to the existence of a monetary union between Belgium and Luxembourg. In this union, the principal responsibility for its management ment is held by Belgium and 95 per cent of the currency in circulation is denominated in Belgian francs.

Despite the existence of this union, differences in the respective banking systems may be observed. Therefore, the systems of the two countries are examined separately.

Belgium.

The situation in the Belgian banking sphere is a somewhat mixed one in which clear limitations are placed on the banks' operations. The situation would seem to be somewhere in between the French and Italian ones ----- though it is quite specifically Belgian. Thus, to give an example, whilst, on the one hand, banks which are constituted in the

✱) These parts are quoted directly from the replies of the Central Bank of Ireland.

form of a commercial company (e.g. with limited liability) are required, by law, to invest a certain amount of their finances in public funds, they are not, on the other hand (with some exceptions), allowed to combine banking with holding activities. In more detail, the precise situation is as follows:

(i) Whilst there exists no specific legislation which obliges Belgian banks to give priority in their lending to the public sector, banks which are constituted as commercial companies are required to keep their legal reserves in the form of securities issued by public authorities. According to the Belgian Banking Commission, banks do in fact hold more than required legal reserves in public securities. Thus, at the end of june 1983, lending to the public sector constituted 39 per cent of total bank lending facilities.

Also, regarding the solvency ratio of banks, where the public sector is concerned, banking regulations are much more generous than for the private sector.

(ii) According to the Belgian Banking Law of 1934, banking and commercial activities may not be mixed. This prohibition only applies to banks constituted in the form of a corporation, and, there are five specific exceptions to this rule. Among these,the most important one does give the Banking Commission the right to allow individual banks to participate in commercial enterprises -- normally activities linked with banking.

(iii) Apart from the prohibition just mentioned in (ii) banks may offer a variety of services to their customers.

(iv) Private financial institutions in Belgian are under no obligation to channel part of their funds through state agencies. However, some institutions such as private savings banks, insurance and capitalisation companies and those granting mortgages (but not banks) are required to invest a certain amount of their funds in public securities.

The banking loans in Belgium do therefore lay down quite clear obligations and limits on the activities of banks and similar financial institutions. The obligations to hold public securities makes the situation in Belgium close to the French one. In contrast, the prohibition of combining banking and commercial activities seems to make Belgium at least as rigid as Italy.

Luxembourg

In Luxembourg, as is stressed in Appendix VI, the banking situation is (particularly when compared with that existing in Belgium) a relatively free one. The precise situation is as follows:

1. Commercial banks are under no obligation to give priority in their lending facilities to the public sector.
2. No legal limits exist concerning the ownership by commercial banks of shares in commercial/industrial enterprises or in holding companies. However banks have to report both actual and planned (plus objectives pursued) participation to the L.M.I. (Luxembourg Monetary Institute).
3. Commercial banks may offer diverse banking and ancillary services to customers - provided that banking activity remains their main one.
4. Private financial institutions are under no obligation to channel part of their funds through State agencies.

Progress in Banking Integration

The account hitherto indicates differences between the banking systems in EEC countries. Also, apart from Luxembourg (and to a certain degree, the City of London), there appears to exist little or no encouragement to inter-Member State penetration by Community Commercial banks. Thus, what, if anything, has been done by the EEC to encourage competition in this area and the establishment of commercial banks across Common Market national frontiers?

The author would, in a few words, answer this question by saying, "surprisingly little". In reality, there have been two legal attempts by the Community at harmonising banking law (whether or not this is the right way to tackle the integration of banking systems will be discussed later in this chapter.

The first attempt was a liberalisation directive (Official Journal, No.L.194,16, July 1973). This directive was to have become effective within 18 months (4 years in the case of the Netherlands) - but was never really applied. Basically speaking, it aimed at prohibiting discriminatory treatment against the establishment of financial institutions from other Member States or against the rendering of services by these institutions in another Member State. This directive also included a sector on the classification of assets.

The next directive (Official Journal, No.L.322.A, December 1977) aimed specifically at the "Co-ordination of Laws, Regulations and Administrative Provisions relating to the Taking-up and Pursuit of Credit Institutions". This directive came into effect in 1980 (in principle, in 1985 or 1989 in the case of Italy). This very, very tame piece of legislation is based on the principle of "equivalence". Thus, a receiving EEC Member State would allow a bank from another (sending) Member State to set up in business in its country provided that it met the legal requirements for authorisation of its own home (sending) Government. However, playing absolutely safe, the Government of the home (sending) country of the bank accepts responsibility for the bank's operations (including financial banking in case of bankruptcy) in the receiving Community country. As was to be expected, this piece of legalistic nonsense has in fact <u>not</u> led to any inter-State penetration within the Common Market by Community commercial banks.

On the positive side, the directive does preconcise a gradual step-by-step harmonisation of banking laws. This part of the legislation has been more effective. In particular, in 1979, the United Kingdom, for the first time in its history passed a series of banking laws to bring the situation in Britain into line with the practices of continental European countries.

Despite this particularly disappointing record in the field of banking (though a little brighter than that concerning the freeing of capital movements and the integration of European capital markets), new proposals have been made regarding financial services. Thus, in january 1981, Commissioner Tugendhat made a call for the linking-up of stock exchanges. Two months later, the Netherlands and the United Kingdom made a call for the freeing of the establishment of insurance companies and the undertaking of insurance business in the EEC. So far, alas, no real progress has been made on either of these fronts.

To the author, the Community would seem to be tackling the situation from too tame a position. Basically, what is really needed is more competition - leading to the provision of better services (though the widening of choice) for the citizens of the EEC - thereby increasing their welfare. Thus, instead of wasting time with all this tame legislation, the Commission should use articles 85 and 86 of the Treaty of Rome - both of which have proved to be redoutable weapons in the field of competition.

NOTES : Part Four.

1. P.Coffey and J.R.Presley, "London and the Development of a European Capital Market", The Bankers' Magazine, London, June 1971.
2. See: Fiscal Integration : Communication from the Commission to the Council, Brussels, 20. April 1983. (Appendix III).
3. These were: the Council Directive which was passed on 11. May 1960 (Official Journal no.921/60, 12. July 1960), implementing article 67 of the Treaty of Rome, relating to the abolition of restrictions on the freedom of intra-EEC capital movements. This Directive was supplemented and amended by a Council Directive (63/21/EEC) on 18. December, 1962 (Official Journal no.62/63 of 22. January, 1963). Unfortunately for the hoped - for freeing of capital movements, the Directive 921/60 contained a safeguard clause (article 3, paragraph 2) allowing states to maintain or reestablish controls over capital movements should a freeing of such movements jeopardise their national policies.
4. EEC Commission, "The Development of a European Capital Market" (The Segré Report), Brussels, 1966.

PART FIVE : The Future of the EMS: Institutional Considerations

Chapter 11 : The European Monetary Fund.

A European Fund for Monetary Co-operation (EFMC) has, as a legal creation, existed since 1973. Unfortunately, at the time of its creation, it was not possible to reach an agreement on the permanent site of the Fund ---- the contestants being London and Luxembourg. Thus the following compromise was agreed upon. The "shadow" of the temporary home of the organ takes the form of a name plate on a building in Luxembourg. However, the EMS is managed by the Commission in Brussels whilst the management of the monetary credits and the ECU's (received by EEC central banks on a three monthly "revolving" basis in exchange for twenty per cent of their reserves of gold and dollars) in the framework of the EMS is the responsibility of the Bank for International Settlements (BIS) in Basel, in Switzerland. Here, the only pre-condition is that the two or three officials managing these matters should be Community officials.

When the EMS was organised, it was hoped that during the course of the review of the workings of the System (planned for March 1981), a decision might be taken both to move on to a second and more advanced stage of integration and to create a "real" Fund. In the event, neither of these hopes materialised and the EMS continued in much the same way as it had done during the first two years of its life. However, developments - outside the official framework of the System - make it now necessary to examine more closely the possible options for transforming the present EFMC into a more concrete and living organ - endowed with real responsibilities. The developments concern the growing use of the ECU's for commercial purposes and the consequent demands made by the commercial banks for the organisation of a clearing union for these units of account. The author would suggest that the Community should avoid the experience with the Euro-Dollar market - over which Member State Governments have little or no control - and bring the commercial market for ECU's firmly under its influence through the transformation of the present EFMC into a really effective organ.

Ideally, in a full EMU (as constructed with the present EMS), the Fund would most probably be a kind of Federal Reserve Board and would be responsible for the creation of ECU's and for open market operations in ECU's. Similarly, it would defend the ECU in international money markets. Inside the Community the Fund would be responsible for controlling liquidity and for monetary policy in general. However, this situation and goal remain future possibilities rather than present realities. Furthermore, even if the EEC were to be so fully integrated as to be conducting over sixty per cent of its trade internally, the choice of the kind of Fund would not be simple, because the different Member States (see: the previous chapter) give varying degrees of independence to their central banks.

Although the Community still finds itself (officially at least) at the first stage of the EMS, there exist many proposals regarding the future position and role for the Fund. At the time of writing, one may discern at least five different points of view: these are, the French attitude, the German view (here, there are in fact two - that of the Government and that of the Bundesbank), the proposals of the EEC's Monetary Committee, the Benelux attitude and that of the Commission of the European Communities. Thus, it is important to examine these different points of view before making proposals which would seem relevant to the present and the immediate future.

The French and German Attitudes.

Received opinion outside France and West Germany give the impression that the two countries hold diametrically opposed views about the form of the future Fund. In reality, the situation is rather ambiguous, and, on a number of points, the two countries do hold rather similar attitudes.

When examining the French and the German attitudes to the Fund, it should be borne in mind that the EMS saw the light of day because of the initiative taken in 1978 by the French President, Giscard D'Estaing, and the German Chancellor, Helmut Schmidt. Therefore, the decision to launch the EMS was a political one. In France, the President's views represented the combined views of the Government, the Ministry of Finance and the Banque de France. Furthermore, the impression was given that in exchange for German support for the French Franc, the French were willingning to support German preferences for a greater co-ordination of national economies. In contrast, Chancellor Schmidt's views represented those of the Government - but not of the Bundesbank. Indeed, the German Central Bank, which has the constitutional right to control monetary policy and inflation, maintains that it was never adequately consulted about the EMS. Furthermore, the Bundesbank has, since the inception of the System, always feared that the Germans would find themselves obliged to intervene excessively in the exchange markets to support other EEC national currencies - thereby increasing inflation in West Germany through the creation of extra Deutsche-marks.

Examining the French attitudes to the future of the Fund, one observes no hard and fast position. Apparently, the French would equally support either a form of regional monetary fund or a fully-fledged European Central Bank. Nevertheless, whatever form the Fund finally takes, the

French do insist that certain relevant factors be taken into account. Thus, both the ECU and gold must be sound and equal to each other. Equally, they must be accepted as a means of settlement and be easily transferable throughout the EEC. At the institutional level, France insists that the Fund's criteria and role must be clearly defined and laid down before anything is institutionalised.

Concerning the question of monetary sovereignty and the ownership of gold and currencies, the French seem to be rather flexible. A willingness is expressed to give up the ownership thereof (presumably transferring it to the Fund) of a part of their reserves - provided that any participating Member State with balance-of-payments problems (and/or similar problems) may draw on the Fund's reserves without having obtained the prior consent of the original country which originally owned the reserves in question. In this sense, the French may be said to go someway beyond the basic idea of a regional monetary fund. Should these views, in reality, be the views of the French Government, then they do represent a significant and novel move in the direction of supranationality. Furthermore, this view suggests the creation of an organ at an international level which differs quite substantially from any other which has hitherto been created.

In West Germany, there exist two different points of view regarding the future role and position of the Fund. Thus, the Government has indicated a preference for a type of regional monetary fund with a limited role for the ECU. The Bundesbank, however, is much stronger and emphatic in its definition of the future Fund. The Bank's officials point out that according to the country's constitution, the Bundesbank plays the major role in the management of the country's monetary policies - also, in contrast with the central banks of other European countries, the Bundesbank is highly independent. Hence, they assume that their countrymen would prefer to see the creation of a highly independent fully-fledged European Central Bank. They support their assumption by the fact that any delegation of powers to such a European institution would necessitate a revision of the West German Constitution. Here, the Bundesbank assumes that the country would only allow its powers to be transferred to a European organ endowed with an equal degree of independence. In this particular choice of a highly independent European Central Bank, the Bundesbank is largely supported by the Netherlands.

On one point, both the West German Government and the Bundesbank are fairly unanimous. Both view the ECU with suspicion and do not wish to give it a legal status inside their country.

This negative attitude is not satisfactorily explained by German officials who do not appear to be aware of the possibility of the ECU taking away some of the frequent strong pressures experienced by the Deutsche Mark in the international currency markets. Despite this rather disappointing attitude towards the ECU, a number of concrete and constructive proposals have nevertheless been made in different parts of the Community for the creation of a "real" Fund.

Specific Proposals for the Fund.

The body which has been making a thorough examination of the future role, both of the ECU and of the Fund, is the Monetary Committee of the EEC. In its Twentieth Report, the Committee undertook an examination (part V of the Report) of the different possibilities open to the Community [1]. It looked at ways of giving the ECU permanency, convertibility and profitability; at ways of consolidating the credit mechanisms; and at the institutional structure and actual working of the Fund. In this last part of the report, the Committee does consider the three possible options for the Fund - as a European Central Bank, as a kind of regional IMF and as something in-between.

The former chairman of the Monetary Committee, Mr. Van Yspersele De Strimon made some striking proposals in the autumn of 1979. Speaking in a personel capacity, he made the following suggestions:

(i) The present "credits exchanged" between the national central banks of the EEC and the embryonic fund should become: (a) "a permanent transfer of 20% of the reserves held in dollars plus an amount in national currency equivalent to 20% of total reserves". (b) Regarding gold, the Central Banks could choose between the present system and permanent transfer. However, the sum transferred or credited would reflect the economic weight of each country.

(ii) "The Fund would supply the Central Banks, in exchange for these transfers, with ECU's which would be: (a) freely useable when created against reserves deposited; (b) 'blocked'. i.e. useable on the basis of 'credit lines' in the short and medium term, when created against national currencies".

(iii) The ECU would have to be completely convertible into third currencies.

(iv) All the credit mechanisms should be consolidated in the Fund.

However, it is on the Report from the Commission (of 20 March 1980) to the European Council on the European Monetary Fund [2], wherein may be found some of the most important Commission proposals on this subject.

In this study, the Commission is particularly concerned with the future credit mechanism - especially with the possibility of the Fund's future ability to create ECU's - as well as with the role of the ECU itself. In this context, the Commission makes the following principal observations.

The Commission seems to criticise [3] the fact that ECU's are not used exclusively in settlement provisions, "since the provisions are without prejudice to other mutually agreed forms of settlement, and as indicated above acceptability is limited to 50% of a claim at the end of the financing period of the VSTF" [4]

To the author, this critical observation raises two issues. One issue concerns the fact that acceptability is limited to 50%. The other concerns the fact of the existence of other "mutually agreed forms of settlement" and the attractiveness of the ECU vis-à-vis these other means. In the former case, it is clear that since the ECU is the Community's official unit of account, then it should be possible to settle debts up 10 100% in ECU's. However, in the latter case, the attractiveness of different means of settlement may work in various ways. It is frequently highly probable that the ECU is so attractive that holders may (acting on Gresham's law) be tempted to hang on to their ECU's and use other currencies. Equally, but more surely, the opposite may happen.

The Commission also critisises the present lack of convertibility of ECU's by the Fund (except for the 20% national holdings of gold and dollars) into other reserve assets. Here, the pressures of commercial banks - and the growing use of the ECU for commercial purposes - will most probably rectify this state of affairs in the relatively near future.

The authorbelieves that the Commission is treading on much weaker ground when it proposes "the ECU would be given the characteristics of acceptability and exclusivity if debts and claims between the central banks had to be denominated and settled in ECU's" Official Community transactions are already denominated and settled in ECU's. It would be quite sufficient for other transactions within the EEC to be "able" to be denominated and settled in ECU's. If, as the author assumes, the ECU is attractive, then its use will automatically expand. Thus, it is not necessary to impose its use on the Community. Nevertheless, those EEC nationals desiring to hold and use ECU's should be given the right to do so.

As the author continually stresses, in the commercial field, the use of the ECU expands unabated, and, therefore, somebody should be responsible for its regulation - and supply. Here, both the Commission and the author agree that this should logically be the responsibility of the Fund. On this point, the other view - raised by the Commission in this document - is the principle of negotiability, i.e. "that transactions should be made mainly with other participants". The Commission (and here, the author is in agreement) notes that the two approaches are not mutually exclusive.

Regarding the negotiability approach, the Commission raises the following very imporant issues:
(i) the question of the adequate supply of ECU's for this somewhat restricted 'market' will be important. Similarly, the question of the yield of the ECU is most relevant.
(ii) should this restricted 'market' be too narrow, the Commission suggests that it should be possible, using a key, to use a designation plan. The key could be "pre-specified or determined on an ad hoc basis according to the circumstances".

Although in its proposals for a designation plan, the Commission at first mentions the use of dollars, the author considers that both national currencies of EEC Member-States and other reserve assets - as well as dollars - should be used - from the beginning - rather than at a later stage.

Turning to other important issues, the Commission suggests that ECU convertibility through the Fund raises two important issues:

"(i) into what should the ECU be convertible and with what ECU's can be acquired, and (ii) according to what rules and conditions?"

The Author's Own Proposals for a "Real" Fund.

At this present moment in time, the author considers that it is not necessary to make the definitive choice for the final type of Fund - such a choice being more of a long-term one. Instead, in the short - to medium-term, there are urgent decisions which should be taken - especially relating to the use of and control over the ECU. Furthermore, the author considers that if the correct decisions are now taken about these questions, then the choice concerning the definitive type of Fund may be easier.

What then are the immediate problems which should be tackled and which according to the author should logically fall within the purview of the Fund? Most of the most urgent questions concern the ECU. Which body should be responsible for control over this unit of account and what form should this control take?

At the present time, as has already been described, the use of the ECU - for commercial purposes - continues to grow. Equally, responsibility for the credits used in the EMS and for the three monthly revolving "swap" arrangements against ECU's is with the BIS in Basel whilst overall responsibility for the management of the EMS remains with the Commission, in Brussels. This is obviously an unsatisfactory situation. Now, because of the increasing non-official use of the ECU, the commercial banks are pressing for the creation of a clearing union for the ECU - and - ECU-dominated travellers' cheques will probably come on stream this year. Most recently, in January, this year, the BIS has been reported as being unwilling to accept responsibility for the organisation of a clearing union for ECU's (see: the Economist, 21 January 1984). The present situation is therefore quite unacceptable.

The Council of Ministers should, therefore, take a definite decision regarding the final site of the Fund - for reasons of the existence of financial expertise, this should preferably be in London. The Fund should be given the following immediate responsibilities:

(i) the "lender of last resort" for the clearing union of ECU's.

(ii) the management of the short- and medium-term credits in the framework of the EMS.

(iii) the management of the three-monthly central bank "revolving" swaps against ECU's.

Also the Fund should be empowered to:

(iv) organise swaps of ECU's against national currencies of the Community Member States,

(v) to organise swaps of ECU's against dollars with the Federal Reserve Board, and,

(vi) to organise emergency supplies of ECU's, EEC national currencies and dollars for EEC Member States facing temporary and sudden shortages of such currencies.

Finally,

(vii) The Fund would be responsible for the future creation of any new issues of ECU's.

The taking of these non-revolutionary decisions by the Council of Ministers would not require any national constitutional changes and would not (as seems to be the fear of a number of central banks) lead to the creation - in even the medium-term - of a European Central Bank. However, these decisions should be taken quickly since there is a danger of a kind of ECU anarchy arising within the Common Market if they are not taken.

The long-term choice about the final type of Fund (e.g. a kind of European IMF or a French or German type of Central Bank) can be taken when the time arrives. Whatever the final version the Fund may take, it will almost certainly be responsible for the following tasks:

(i) open market operations in ECU's,

(ii) intervention operations in the international money markets to maintain the parity of the ECU at agreed levels,

(iii) the taking of policy decisions regarding the position of the ECU, and, most probably,

(iv) the making of proposals to the governments of Community Member States regarding their national economic, fiscal and monetery policies.

These are all major responsibilities and would confer on the Fund an importance which most central banks would, at the present time, be loathe to relinguish. The author believe that it will be the force of events - due mainly to the attractiveness of the ECU and to its increasing use for commercial purposes which will force governments eventually to transfer real power to the Fund. Although, at the present tim grandiose plans for the creation of a European Central Bank are really quite unnecessary, there are a number of urgent decisions concerning the management of the ECU and the role of the Fund which should preferably be taken as soon as possible. Logically, responsibility for the management of the ECU should be given to a "real" European Fund.

PART FIVE.

Chapter 11.

Footnotes

1. See: Twentieth Report of the Activities of the Monetary Committee. Official Journal of the European Communities. No.C 240/1, 25. September 1979.

2. Originally published in European Economy, Number 7, November 1980: Chapter 6 of the Annual Economic Review 1980 - 1981.

3. See: European Economy, Number 7, cited:2.

4. VSTF : Very Short Term Financial Facilities.

Part Six: Other Present and Future EEC Member States.

Chapter 12 : The United Kingdom.

The experience of the United Kingdom in the old "Snake" Arrangement was indeed a traumatic one. In the space of a few weeks, the country lost about a third of its reserves of foreign currencies through its intervention in the exchange markets. The British then left the arrangement - never to return again.

When, in 1978, the initial discussions took place between the French and Germans about the possibility of creating an EMS, Britain viewed such a development with the greatest suspicion - fearing a repetition of the experience of the EMS's predecessor when new Member States had been presented with a fait accompli. Furthermore the British always feared that membership of something like an EMS would severely restrict the country's freedom in managing its national economic policy. More specifically, it was felt that the country had to maintain its freedom to change the value of the Pound Sterling - should this be necessary. A body of opinion (particularly the members of the Cambridge School) considered that occasional well-timed devaluations of the national currency would lead to the possibility of supporting employment.

When, in 1979, a Conservative Government came to power in Britain, exchange controls were swept aside and, like the participants of the EMS, Britain exchanged 20 per cent of its holdings of gold and dollars against ECU's (on a 'revolving' 3 monthly swap basis). But, still, the United Kingdom did not join the EMS - why not? Officially, the argument always made has been that since Pound Sterling was now an oil currency, speculation in favour of the British currency would place too great a strain on the EMS should Britain join. More recently, however, partly as a result of the international oil glut and the high value of the U.S.Dollar, the value of the Pound Sterling has tended to decline. But still, despite repeated calls from the

EC Commission and other Member States, the British have remained outside the System. To some observers, this is strangebecause Britain is one of the most fervent supporters of the principal public economic policy choice shared by all EEC countries (except Greece) - namely, the control of inflation.
Writing in 1981 [1)] Geoffrey Dennis questioned whether "conventional analysis of the degree of independent control over monetary policy in flexible as opposed to fixed exchange rate arrangements is correct, both in abstract form, and with respect to the EMS in particular, UK membership of it". In his paper, he concluded that "membership of the EMS would involve the U.K. in little loss of monetary autonomy compared to its experience as a non-member and that therefore this argument against joining the EMS is significantly outweighed by the benefits of membership". The main evidence given for this conclusion lies in the fact that the existence of an automatic sterilisation mechanism for the U.K. money supply (through institutional factors) means that the country does not lose complete monetary autonomy under fixed exchange rates. Nevertheless, this freedom seems to be guaranteed for Britain alone - or together with some others - but of everyone tried to participate this "deliberate sterilisation" together - the EMS would break down.
To the author, in the specific case of the United Kingdom, the consideration of monetary independence is no longer an important one. The main reasons for this observation are:
(i) the British Government now fervently espouses the main public economic policy choice shared by all, but one, EEC Member States, namely: the control of inflation. Therefore, membership of the EMS should help to facilitate the task of the British Government.
(ii) Since Britain has now removed exchange controls, she, in this field, joins the league of such countries as West-Germany.
(iii) Exchange Rates within the EMS are stable, but NOT fixed, thus, should adjustments be necassary, they may be made.
(iv) Britain has already exchanged 20 per cent of her reserves of gold and dollars against ECU's, therefore, it would be reasonable to fully join the System.
(v) The value of the Pound Sterling is now at a relatively low level - compared with a year or two ago. Britain's membership of the EMS would

therefore not cause tensions. Should the United Kingdom join and should the international value of the British currency rise - causing tensions within the System - then the necessary adjustments may be made.
The author, then, considers that the situation concerning the United Kingdom is now radically different from that which existed in 1972 - or even in 1978. According to the five afore-mentioned reasons, Britain could now join the EMS without causing problems for herself - or her partners in the EEC.

Chapter 13 : The New Member States

When examining the possible implications of the EMS for New Member States, it is, at the outset, important to note that no country in the Common Market is under any obligation whatsoever to join the EMS. Thus, in this context neither Greece nor the United Kingdom are members of the System. Consequently, the relevant questions which should be considered when examining the case of new Member States are:

(i) what advantages, if any, could a new Member State hope to obtain in joining the EMS?

(ii) What structural conditions might such countries have to fulfill in order to join?

(iii) Once having joined the EMS, what might be the internal economic policy conditions/constraints which such countries have to accept?

The Possible Advantages of Joining the EMS.

The EMS has proved itself to be a zone of international monetary stability, and, most economists would agree that exchange-rate fluctuations among the participating countries have been much less than they might have been had the System not existed. Thus, a new Member State on joining the EMS would also join this zone of monetary stability.

As an integral part of participation, a country would find its currency supported by its partners. As a counterpart to this, the country concerned would find itself under pressure to support its own currency when fluctuations reached the relevant limits vis-à-vis the ECU.

Whilst a participant undertakes the responsibility to intervene in the exchange markets to support its own currency, it would have access to the rather generous credits of the Community should it face balance-of-payments or similar problems. Furthermore, it is highly probable that the Community would (as was done for Ireland and Italy) organise interest rate subsidies for loans for such countries.

The Structural Factors.

There are two important structural factors which deserve serious consideration by new Member States contemplating membership of the EMS.

One of these factors concerns trade, the other, the economic policy choice of the countries concerned.

At the trade structural level, the factor which has to be examined is the degree to which the economy of a prospective member is an open one and the proportion of its GNP which is traded with the EEC. This is really a most fundamental consideration because of a country's economy is not open and if it is trading only a modest amount of its GNP with other Community Member States, then, there will be little demand for the currencies of the different partners - and consequently - little point in linking them together. This, however, may well change at the end of the transitional phase when a new Member State would (economically and financially) become a full Member. At such a moment, much more of the country's trade may be transacted within the Community itself and it may wish to re-examine the question of its possible participation in the EMS.

The public economic policy choice of a prospective Member State is of critical importance when contemplating possible participation in the EMS. Among all the present members of the System, the common policy element is the control of inflation. This policy choice is absolutely pre-eminent. A country which did not already or could not consider subscribing to this policy choice should not even consider joining the EMS. Such is clearly the position of Greece.

Economic Policy Conditions or Constraints

The preceding paragraph contains the real constraining policy choice for new Member States considering joining the EMS. As the experience of present participants has amply confirmed, the overriding public economic policy choice of participants is the control of inflation. Thus, future participants would, sooner or later, find any other economic policy choices (such as excessive economic expansion, for example) considerably reduced.

There are quite clear policy implications for prospective participants in the EMS. Thus, when their currency fluctuations reach the limits of the band of intervention vis-ã-vis the ECU, they must intervene. If currency exchange intervention does not settle matters, then both exchange rate adjustments and internal policy action must be contemplated and probably undertaken.

It is, of course, important to note that exchange rate adjustments are an integral part of the System - consequently, this very important policy weapon still remains in the economic policy armoury of participants. Nevertheless, this weapon is not intended to be used in an arbitrary fashion.

The most important policy choice which future members are forced to bear in mind is the control of inflation. In the short to medium term, these countries have to accept this aim --- this fact automatically qualifies or disqualifies, in advance, certain countries as possible members of the System.

Possible Candidates

Apart from the United Kingdom, already a full member of the EEC and whose position was examined in the preceding chapter, there are three countries which could possibly consider membership of the EMS. These countries are Greece, Portugal and Spain.

Greece is already a Community Member State, and, by the end of next year (1985), the Greek currency, the Drachma, will become an integral component of the ECU. Thus, Greece could consider becoming a member of the EMS. Unfortunately, Greece clearly does not accept the control of inflation as a public economic policy choice. Indeed, as statistics (in table no. 6 in the Conclusions of this work) indicate, the Greek level of inflation is so great when compared with that of other Member States that Greece could not, at the present time, seriously consider membership of the EMS.

Turning to Portugal and Spain, the perspectives could be different from that of Greece. Should the negotiations leading to accession proceed favourably, it is expected that Portugal and Spain will join the Community by the end of 1986. However, both countries would enjoy a period of transition at the end of which time (unlikely to happen before the end of this period) the Escudo and the Peseta will become component parts of the ECU. Normally, this would be the moment for these countries to seriously consider joining the EMS. So, what are the prospectives for these two countries?

In principle, at the present time, both these countries aim to control, and preferably, to bring down their levels of inflation. Thus, in principle, they have accepted the same public economic policy choice as all the present EEC Member States (except Greece). However, they are by no means as successful as most of the present countries of the Common Market in controlling inflation. This fact implies that it is not enough to accept the same economic policy choice as the present Member States - it is essential that inflation rates actually fall and even converge. Since, however, it will be a number of years before the question of EMS membership for Portugal and Spain becomes a real possibility, both countries can look forward to a substantial breathing space in which to really transform their economic choice into a practical reality.

Notes : Part Six.

1. G.E.J.Dennis, "U.K. Monetary Independence and Membership of the E.M.S.", in "European Monetary System and International Monetary Reform", Editions de l"Université de Bruxelles, 1981.

PART Seven : Non-Community Countries.

Chapter 14. - The United States and Japan and Third World Countries.

In April, this year (1984), Soviet bankers made a call for a wider role for the ECU [1].

At the end of the delivery of a paper on the EMS, by the author, in Washington D.C., in October 1983, an important United States official expressed his fears for the future of the "privileged" position of the US Dollar should the ECU become strong [2].

Both these statements confirm the author's long-standing conviction that the "ECU is foredoomed to be successful" [3]. However, this success will not come about overnight and its position has to be defined not only in relation to the US Dollar, the Japanese Yen, the Swiss Franc - to name the three main competitors (apart from the Deutsche Mark and the Pound Sterling) - but also in relation to Third World Countries.

But, first, what can and should be the relationship between the ECU and the US Dollar, the Japanese Yen and the Swiss Franc? The immediate answer is that it has to be convertible into these currencies. At the moment, directly speaking, this convertibility does not exist. Therefore, the Community should negotiate an agreement (including "swap" agreements with the Federal Reserve Board and the Central Bank of Japan) instituting just such a convertibility with the United States, Japan, Switzerland and similar countries.

At the moment, the ECU is stable (there has been no exchange rate adjustment since March 1983). This stability is probably due to four main factors, these are:

(i) rates of inflation among EEC Member States have, in 1983, fallen, sometimes substantially, and, in some cases, have tended to converge (see: table No.6 (Conclusions),

(ii) where necessary, the System's participants have intervened successfully in the currency markets to stabilise their currencies, and

(iii) the strength of the US Dollar has tended to weaken the Deutsche Mark. In turn, this has reduced tensions between Community currencies which a strong German currency might have caused.

(iv) Although not a member of the EMS, a strong British currency might have caused tensions within the System. The recent weakness of the Pound Sterling vis-à-vis the US Dollar has therefore removed this possible source of tension.

The question that must now be asked is, how, if at all, can this stability of the ECU be maintained? The answer lies in the continued reduction in and convergence of Community inflation rates and in a possible convergence of EEC interest rates. This is absolutely essential, since, when the value of the US Dollar falls (as it surely must do after the US presidential elections), then "hot" money will tend to flow towards European "hard" currencies and towards the Japanese Yen. Thus, if the attractiveness of all (or nearly all) EEC currencies is fairly equal, then, the ECU should be attractive - particularly should it be convertible. Naturally, the position of the EMS and the ECU could be reinforced both internally and internationally by the creation of a "real" European Monetary Fund.

To the author, the ECU should reflect the Community's economic and trading position internationally. Equally, the ECU should be accorded some of the present international rights of "seignorage" at present enjoyed almost exclusively by the US Dollar. All this implies that the ECU should become an important international trading currency. In turn, this implies the conclusion of agreements with a large number of countries in the Third World. Such agreements could be highly beneficial to both sides.

Third World Countries

In conversations with friends and colleagues in Third World countries, the author has expressed surprise that their countries should nearly always link their currencies with the US Dollar. This surpise is based on the fact that in many cases, it is the Community which is the most important trading partner for these countries. Thus, for example, in Brazil, it is the Community which is that country's most important trading partner and foreign investor. Consequently, according to the author, the Brazilians should link the Cruzeiro to the ECU.

Apart from consideration of trade (which are of mutual interest to both the Community and Third World countries) there is, for Third World countries, the major consideration of the stability and relatively low interest rates associated with the ECU. Should this situation continue, it could become very attractive for Third World countries to borrow ECU's. Their dreadful experience with international debts denominated in dollars, should encourage them to turn to the ECU. The author would like to make the following proposals for linking the ECU to currencies of Third World Countries:

(i) the Community should conclude agreements with Third World countries to denominate their exports (particularly of raw materials and energy) to the EEC in ECU's.

(ii) The Community should, preferably before the conclusion of such agreements, make the ECU convertible.

(iii) The EEC should study the possibility of organising a Community - Third World monetary system (using the ECU) based on the example of the French Franc Zone.

(iv) Similarly, the possibility of making the Stabex System (using the ECU) more international should be examined.

The Overall View.

To the author, the world should, logically, evolve into a number of monetary zones - each reflecting the economic, commercial and trading strengths of the countries represented by the currencies. Thus, in an international monetary system made up of "convertible" currencies, the most logical major zones would be the US Dollar, the Japanese Yen and the ECU ones. It is really now high time that the Community take steps to translate the ECU trading and monetary zone into an international reality.

Notes: Part Seven.

1. See: Financial Times, 18. April, 1984.
2. See: P.Coffey, "The Open International Economy - The Reaction of the EEC - The European Monetary System - An Attempt at Further Integration", Occasional Papers of the Europa Instituut, Nr.4, University of Amsterdam, 1984.
3. See: P.Coffey (Editor), "Main Economic Policy Areas of the EEC", Nijhoff, Den Haag, 1983.

Part Eight: The Future of the EMS - Towards an EMU?

Chapter 15 : Basic Considerations.

Until this moment, basic technical considerations and the question of other Member States joining the EMS have dominated this work, and yet, as the author stated in the preface, the EMS should be seen in a larger historical context as a transition on the way to a full EMU. Is this, then, a realistic assumption? If so, how will this transformation come about? If not, what might happen to the EMS?

Certainly, the EMS will not, of its own accord, become an EMU, but, if it continues to be as successful as it has been during the first five years of its existence, then it is highly probable that foundations will be laid which will allow an EMU to be constructed. Rightly or wrongly, all the Member States of the EEC (with the exception of Greece) have, for the first time in decades, opted for the same economic public policy choice, namely, the control of inflation. This is really very important bacause, apart from the fact that almost all of these countries are now on the same wavelength, if they succeed in making their inflation rates converge, then exchange rate speculation and fluctuations will tend to disappear. Consequently, it would be possible to remove controls over capital movements and exchange rates. In turn, the stage would be set for the integration of capital markets and competition for savings.

Naturally, the construction of an EMU would require definite structural moves by Common Market countries since the freeing of controls would in themselves not be enough. At least in three areas, the Community would have to consciously make structural policy choices. Thus first, official Community resources should be directed towards future real needs rather than to wasteful out-of-date policies. Here, the current decision to reduce financial resources for the dairy sector of the CAP and to channel them more towards advanced technology (i.e. the Esprit Project) is a move in the right direction. Second, changes in social security policies should be made in order to remove the present inflexibility in the labour market and to induce labour mobility. Third, a really active Community regional policy has to be devised. These three policy areas are the absolute minimum for Community activity and the author automatically assumes that the adoption of many dynamic policies will be necessary. Nevertheless, the present concern about inflation does mean that the stage is now set for a liberalisation of controls - leading to the adoption of dynamic Community policies.

The eventuality must not be excluded, that, in reality, whatever may be said in public, most governments among the Common Market countries do not really wish to create a full EMU. Should this eventuality materialise, what is likely to happen to the EMS?

Without any conscious intervention or policy decisions being taken by national or Community authorities, the author suspects that the EMS will develop into something between the present system and a full EMU. Unless there is a major unforeseen economic and/or political upheaval in Europe and/or in the rest of the world, then inflation rates are likely to fall, and, in some cases, to converge. Automatically, the exchange markets would become more stable and controls would be removed since they would have no further raison d'être.

A parallel development is likely to be a further use of the ECU - for commercial purposes. It is the success of this parallel Community currency that is most likely to force the hand of the authorities. On the one hand, it is most likely that a "real" European Monetary Fund will be created ------ which could be the basis for a full European Central Bank should a full EMU be created. On the other hand, the combination of the increasing use of the ECU - together with an easing of controls - would almost certainly lead towards moves in the direction of the creation of an integrated capital market.

There is, of course, yet a further eventuality. Present Member States ---- but, more especially, future ones ---- may decide that they wish to develop economically slower or more quick speeds. This could lead (but at a more advanced level) to a repetition of the old Snake Arrangement whereby a core of countries with similar levels of inflation would integrate more swiftly. Other countries would integrate slowly - with the possibility of joining the fast-growing core of Member States at a later date.

The Author's Proposals for an Economic and Monetary Union

The author has just outlined the absolute minimum requirements which have to be met if it is intended to transform the present EMS into an EMU. It is now necessary to go even further and to make more concrete and detailed suggestions for such a transformation. Without wishing to make an arbitrary list of preferences, the author would suggest that there are five areas of action where both more immediate as well as longer term Community action is necessary. These areas are the technical ones, organisational and credit considerations, budgetary changes and fiscal integration, regional and transport policies and legal changes.

Technical Proposals

Now that all Community Member States, except one, have adopted the same public economic policy choice in the control of inflation, there are strong possibilities that intra-Community exchange-rate speculation will diminish. As soon as concrete signs of such a development become apparent, steps should be taken to make inter-State capital movements within the EEC more easy and to integrate capital markets.

Even without such a development, steps could very quickly be taken to increase competition between banks and to encourage the setting up of branches in EEC States of banks originally domiciled in any single country. The present situation is quite unacceptable and simply tends to maintain the quasi monopolistic power of the commercial banks and to diminish consumer welfare.

But then, two other urgent and important technical considerations are the future use of the ECU and a common definition of the money supply among Community countries. Regarding the ECU, the Commission should use its powers of persuation to encourage all Community Member States to allow their nationals to hold ECU-denominated bank accounts. Also, between Common Market countries it should be possible for all official inter-State debts to be settled in ECU's. Equally, at a practical level, both travellers' cheques (denominated in ECU's) as well as ECU coins should be put into circulation.

The question of a common definition of the money supply is more complex than that of the ECU. In the latter case, the unit of account already exists and the only problem is that of either restraining or encouraging the growing demand for it. The case of the definition of the money supply implies not only agreement on a common definition - but also on the institutions covered by government control of the money supply. Thus, the author would suggest that immediate studies should be undertaken on these matters by competent bodies.

Organisational and Credit Considerations

Two recent developments call for the taking of immediate action in the organisational field. One development is the growing use of the ECU. This implies that either an existing body should be transformed into an organisation endowed with responsibilities for managing the ECU (particularly concerning the role of a clearing union and the management of government "swaps") or that a new organisation should be created for this body. To the author, the easiest and most obvious choice here would be to transform the present phantom European Fund for Monetary Co-operation into a "real" and active Fund. Also, once transformed, the Fund should be given a permanent home - preferably in London because of the wealth of financial expertise in that city. Nothing would, of course, exclude the setting-up of branch offices of the Fund in other Community capitals.

The question of credits (which should also be managed by the Fund) has now become one of "burning actuality". In its Communication to the Council on Financial Integration, in April 1983 (see: Appendix IV), the Commission complained that the Community's credits and financial possibilities had, since 1977, not been used. Since, the transmission of this opinion, things have changed. In particular, following the floating of the "jumbo" loan by the Community in the financial markets, on behalf of France, in 1983, two-thirds of the so-called Ortoli Facility have been used up. Thus, it would now seem necessary to increase these facilities.

Budgetary Changes and Fiscal Integration

Any future moves towards the transformation of the EMS into an EMU will require finances which imply an enlargement of the Community Budget. Equally, any moves in the direction of the freeing of inter-State capital movements and the establishment of services and companies between Common Market countries will automatically require a much greater degree of fiscal integration than is presently the case.

Reference has already been made to the decision (a correct one, the author would say) taken by the Council of Ministers, in 1984, to attempt to reduce the amount of Community financial resources devoted to agriculture. Similarly, they agreed to make available resources for the Community advanced technological project - known as Esprit. However, these moves should go much further. But such moves could well mean expanding the financial resources of the Community Badget. Several proposals have been made about this matter. Thus, for example, the present notional 1 per cent of VAT (known as the Community's own resources or "resources propres") might (albeit in the face of the strong objections of Britain and West Germany) be increased. Otherwise, the resources devoted to existing policies (notably, agriculture) might be reduced further. Another proposal (already made by the Commission) might be the institution of a Community energy tax. Yet another possibility could be the use of a Community Corporation Tax. Such a move would form an integral part of fiscal integration - which is an indispensable part of any process leading to the implementation of a full EMU.

To date, in the field of fiscal integration, all the EEC Member States have adopted the Value Added Tax (VAT), using a destination principal. The next moves in this area would (unlikely to be envisaged in the immediate future) be the harmonisation of VAT at the same levels for the same products - perhaps then moving over to the use of an origin principle.

Some progress has also been made in the field of excise duties. However, although different draft directives have been issued for the implementation of a Community Corporation Tax, so far (though success now appears to be near), no such Common Market tax has emerged. Apart from the necessity of achieving tax neutrality - and thereby facilitating inter-State establishment by EEC enterprises - this tax could be used as a basis for obtaining additional Community financial resources.

Regional and Transport Policy Considerations

Without the implementation of a really effective EEG regional policy - together with the creation of a dynamic Community regional organ - it is difficult to imagine how a number of Community countries (notably those situated on the geographical periphery of the Common Market) could contemplate joing a full EMU. Perhaps, the Italian and West German proposals for their own regional problems might serve as ideal aims or models for a future Community Regional Policy. In the case of Italy, the aim is to channel resources to regions thus enabling them to support facilities (e.g. a university) normally associated with a highly developed area. Similarly - though rather more ambitious in its aims - the Germans, using a highly sophisticated system of regional statistics, intend to provide all citizens with certain basic economic, cultural and social facilities. Should either or both models be adopted by the Community, major financial resources would be needed.

At a dynamic institutional level, perhaps the most useful Community organ would, as Giovanni Magnifico proposed over ten years ago, the setting up of a Community Regional Bank, based on the model of the postwar German Reconstruction Bank.

Similarly, the natural complement to regional policy is a transport policy. Although the Community has not made any monumental progress in the field of regional policy, in contrast, the progress in the field of transport has been absolutely zero. Finally, in the spring of the present year, 1984, progress has, for the first time, been made in the field of transport. This development is particularly important as a step in the direction of an EMU since it will inevitably lead to an increase in competition.

Legal Considerations

Despite the author's doubts about the effectiveness of the banking directives, there is one area where legal progress must be made - if the Community is to facilitate the right of establishment and the creation of an EMU. This area is the provision of a European Company Law. A draft directive to this end has, in fact, been on the table for a number of years. Its enactment now becomes a matter of urgent necessaty - since without it non-Community enterprises will continue to find establishment in Common Market countries than do Community businesses.

Overall Observations

A number of proposals (which in themselves are by no means exhaustive) have been made which should help to facilitate the transformation of the EMS into a full EMU. However, even if inflation rates continue to fall (and even to converge) among Common Market countries, a number of states may not desire to join such a union - prefering the present monetary arrangement. Thus, one could envisage the possibility of some Community countries integrating more swiftly and intensively than others. Nevertheless, the author considers that conditions have never been so favourable for the implementation of a full EMU.

The author is not so sure that most governments in the EEC are favourably disposed to such a development. Should this be the case, the growing attractiveness and use of the commercial ECU would almost inevitably lead to the transformation of the present EMS into something halfway between the present system and a full EMU.

Conclusions

The Overview.

In the preface to this book the author wrote, "the European Monetary System is perhaps the only success story of the Common Market since the First Enlargement". Now, having examined this vast panorama of the EMS - its past, the present and its future - the author is convinced that the EMS (and particularly the ECU) is indeed the "real" success story of the Community since 1972. What are the author's reasons for daring to make such a charged judgement about just one of the many policy areas of the EEC? There are, in fact, quite a number of reasons why such a judgement is appropriate; among which the main ones are:

(i) the EMS has become "the" zone of international monetary stability in the world.

(ii) This stability has been reinforced by the most laudable record in inflation levels in the EEC between 1981 and 1983 (see: Table No.6).

(iii) The record on inflation is due mainly to the fact that, for the first time since the beginning of the Common Market, all the Member States (except one) have adopted the same public economic policy choice, namely, the control of inflation.

(iv) The ECU, apart from being the second reserve asset in the world, has also become the third unit of account for international commercial bond issues.

This is indeed a notable record and is only tarnished by two major defects. First, not all Community Nationals may hold ECU-denominated bank accounts. Second, a "real" European Monetary Fund has not been created, and, consequently, the Community has not moved on to a more advanced stage of integration (at least not officially). These defects should be remedied as soon as possible. Before making final proposals for future improvements in the System, however, it is worth examining the principal reasons for the success of the EMS - and especially of the ECU.

Possible Reasons for the Success of the EMS and the ECU.

The success of the EMS as a zone of monetary stability is mainly

Table No.6

The Success of the EMS.

Inflation Rates

	percentage change over previous year.	
	1981	1983
Belgium	7.6	7.7
Denmark	10.7	6.7
France	12.5	9.3
Germany (West)	5.9	3.2
Greece	24.4	20.0
Ireland	20.5	10.5
Italy	19.0	14.2
Netherlands	6.7	2.8
United Kingdom	10.7	5.5

Source: Eurostat and EC Commission.

Table No.7

ECU Bonds
(at the end of 1983)

Country/Institution	Number of Issues	Volume (M₤)
Italy	6	1,905
France	18	997.2
Ireland	3	90
Netherlands	3	145
Belgium	1	70
W.Germany	1	50
Denmark	1	75
Norway	2	70
Sweden	4	190
U.S.	5	151
Canada	4	225
Japan	3	120
Australia	1	50
South Africa	1	40
Other	1	100
EEC Institutions	17	1,049
Other Europ. Instit.*)	3	90
International Instit.	1	150
Total	75	5,567.2

*) Council of Europe Resettlement Fund

Source: ECU Newsletter, Istituto Bancario San Paolo Di Torino, March 1984.

the result of the serious measures being undertaken by all Member States (except Greece) in trying to reduce their budget deficits and consequently inflation levels. In some cases, notably in Belgium, the Government is taking strong if not draconian measures to bring down the level of inflation. But even with the adoption of such policies - accompanied by necessary exchange rate intervention - it is doubtful whether the EMS could have had such a successful record. To the author, the secret probably lies in the fact that, in comparison with its predecessor, the present System has managed to avoid internal tensions through discreet, swift and appropriate exchange rate adjustments.

The overall success record of the EMS may be relatively easy to explain - that of the ECU is perhaps less clear. But, first, how many different types of ECU are there? The author has discovered two different official ECU's. One is the ECU which is used as the official unit of account of the European Communities. This unit is used for all official Community transactions, such as transfers of development aid, regional aid and the like. The other ECU is that used in the EMS which is the official one - less the Pound Sterling component. Then, of course, there is the commercial ECU used in bank accounts and the one used for international commercial bond issues.

The attractiveness of the ECU lies in its inbuilt safety factor as a risk spreader. The ECU also has the advantage of being backed by the great economic strength of the EEC. To these two factors must be added the particularly important commercial price advantage of borrowing ECU's rather than other important currencies. When examining tables nos. 8 to 11 (inclusive), it is clear that if one takes the arithmetical mean for the period October 1979 to December 1983, then, it was clearly more attractive to borrow ECU's in all countries rather than borrow the three leading international currencies, namely, the US Dollar, the Japanese Yen and the Pound Sterling. More rencently, for the whole of 1983, this situation has continued in the case of the Japanese Yen and has been reinforced vis-à-vis the Dollar. Equally, it has become more attractive to borrow ECU's than either Swiss or French Francs. The position of the Pound Sterling has, however, become erratic.

How many commercial ECU's are there in existence? This is a question frequently asked by students and monetary experts. According to table no. 7, there were in existence at the end of 1983, 5,567,2 million ECU's in bonds. More recently, according to the Commission, there were

THE ADVANTAGES OF BORROWING ECU's

Table No.8 - Effective cost of 6 month indebtedness (on annual basis)
(arithmetical mean - October 1979-December 1983)

Debitor country / Euro-currency	U.S.A.	Germany	Japan	Switzer-land	Great Britain	France	Italy	Belgium	Denmark	Nether-lands
$	13.63	23.78	16.50	21.12	24.10	31.03	31.60	30.16	29.82	24.41
DM	0.43	8.78	2.81	6.28	9.68	15.57	16.16	14.78	14.55	9.33
Yen	6.89	16.42	7.87	13.55	16.39	23.13	23.82	22.27	21.89	16.99
SFR	0.47	8.80	2.52	5.87	9.83	15.59	16.23	14.78	14.47	9.32
UKL	5.10	14.31	7.29	11.91	13.71	21.02	21.67	20.29	20.11	14.81
FF	1.14	9.48	3.28	6.97	10.22	16.13	16.80	15.39	15.23	10.02
ECU	1.45	9.95	3.71	7.46	10.54	16.68	17.30	15.90	15.71	10.48

Table No. 9- Effective cost of 6 month indebtedness (on annual basis)
(standard deviation - October 1979-December 1983)

Debitor country / Euro-currency	U.S.A.	Germany	Japan	Switzer-land	Great Britain	France	Italy	Belgium	Denmark	Nether lands
$	2.95	16.97	20.10	19.41	18.95	18.95	17.53	19.34	16.63	17.98
DM	15.21	2.16	21.49	9.05	17.68	7.95	5.80	9.35	6.35	3.29
Yen	19.57	23.15	1.61	22.16	21.35	21.82	22.17	21.94	19.55	23.50
SFR	18.56	10.45	20.86	2.39	22.16	13.35	13.26	14.03	10.47	10.27
UKL	16.85	18.34	20.43	21.64	2.35	17.27	17.09	18.86	18.11	17.75
FF	16.26	4.99	20.07	9.85	16.50	4.08	4.33	7.86	6.57	4.98
ECU	14.17	3.82	19.60	10.05	13.90	5.97	3.98	7.87	5.54	3.50

Source: ECU Newsletter, Istituto Bancario San Paolo Di Torino, March 1984

THE ADVANTAGES OF BORROWING ECU's

Table No. 10 - Effective cost of 6 month indebtedness (on annual basis)
(arithmetical mean - January-December 1983)

Debitor country / Euro-currency	U.S.A.	Germany	Japan	Switzer-land	Great Britain	France	Italy	Belgium	Denmark	Nether-lands
$	10.37	18.47	1.72	12.28	23.69	26.71	24.80	23.19	21.70	20.60
DM	-0.67	6.46	-9.41	0.69	12.32	14.28	12.50	10.95	9.51	8.55
Yen	16.37	24.10	6.80	17.81	30.44	32.55	30.65	28.98	27.40	26.37
SFR	2.80	10.18	-6.01	4.25	15.89	18.10	16.30	14.75	13.28	12.28
UKL	-1.30	6.77	-9.07	0.82	10.72	14.64	12.72	11.22	9.83	8.77
FF	3.40	10.71	-5.50	4.82	16.68	18.61	16.84	15.29	13.82	12.81
ECU	0.37	7.72	-8.24	1.89	13.27	15.57	13.77	12.23	10.79	9.80

Table No. 11 - Effective cost of 6 month indebtedness (on annual basis)
(standard deviation - January-December 1983)

Debitor country / Euro-currency	U.S.A.	Germany	Japan	Switzer-land	Great Britain	France	Italy	Belgium	Denmark	Nether-lands
$	1.37	10.09	10.79	8.61	12.13	11.17	9.50	9.72	10.25	8.85
DM	11.48	1.35	3.73	4.09	21.01	5.09	2.90	2.03	1.66	3.47
Yen	13.10	3.95	0.45	4.42	22.89	5.60	4.68	4.57	3.61	5.25
SFR	9.63	3.53	3.53	0.60	18.79	4.58	2.91	3.61	3.37	2.83
UKL	9.76	18.88	18.45	16.82	0.96	20.71	18.68	18.82	19.33	18.30
FF	11.66	3.88	4.88	5.21	21.73	2.85	3.29	4.26	4.02	3.34
ECU	8.15	2.68	4.88	2.99	17.37	5.28	2.06	2.37	3.03	2.53

Source: ECU Newsletter, Istituto Bancario San Paolo Di Torino, March 1984.

(in May 1984) ten billions ECU's in bank deposits. At the end of 1979, ECU's constituted 14.6 per cent of official Western reserves.

The attractiveness of the ECU continues unabated and is likely to do so even more as the US Dollar comes under renewed pressure as a result of American economic and monetary mismanagement. An increased importance of the ECU internationally raises the critical and pertinent question of the future place of the ECU within the Common Market itself. To the author, this question should be regarded as a matter of high priority.

The Immediate Future of the ECU within the EEC.

Pascal Salin [1)]has proposed that the Community citizens should be given the opportunity of being able to use whichever currency they choose inside the Common Market. Whilst tha author would not perhaps go quite as far as his French colleague, he would nevertheless insist that the ECU should not only be used (where governments so desire) to settle any national debts within the EEC - but also that all citizens should be allowed to open ECU bank accounts. Similarly, both ECU denominated travellers-cheques (hopefully, soon to become a reality) and a number of ECU coins should be issued. All these moves also imply the making of some institutional changes within the Common Market.

The Institutional Changes.

The increasing use of the ECU for commercial purposes makes the creation of a clearing union a matter of urgent necessity. The author is, alas, painfully aware of the shocked surprise privately being registered by most of the Governments of the Member States of the Community at the success of the ECU. This state of shock - accompanied by their absolute lack of enthusiasm (to put things mildly) for the creation of any "real" monetary organ - has prompted them to petition the Bank for International Settlements (B.I.S.) in Basel, Switzerland, to accept the role of the clearing union for ECU's [2)]. The excuse is that since the B.I.S. is already managing the credits and the "revolving" ECU swap arrangements for the Community, it could, logically (!) also become the clearing union for ECU's. Happily, to date, the B.I.S. (quite rightly, the author would say) does not want to be saddled with any more Community tasks. Exactly, why should it do any more work for the EEC? The B.I.S. is not a Community organ whilst Switzerland is not even an EEC Member State. The audacity of the Governments of the Member States is quite outrageous.

Now, and really now is the time to create the "real" Monetary Fund. Since there is no need whatsoever to create a central bank at this present moment in time, it can be a clearing union and the organ responsible for managing the Community's credits and the ECU "swaps" - as well as making any new issues of ECU's. As, in the future, its responsibilities increase, then, it can be transformed. There is no shortage of proposals and plans for the final version of the Fund. Since, however, we have not even arrived at the second stage of the EMS - let alone a full EMU - the Governments of the Member States should not imagine that they are about to loose their sovereign monetary virginity in creating a "Real" Fund. After all, that was lost long ago to the International Monetary Fund (IMF).

The Technical Moves.

A matter of almost equal urgency and necessity is the question of freeing capital movements between Member States, of increasing competition between banks thereby improving the services offered to Community citizens (thus improving their welfare) and of creating a European Capital Market. As this book has shown, the monetary stability achieved within the Common Market over the past fifteen months implies that there are now real hopes for the freeing of capital movements.

These technical changes should also be accompanied by certain legal and fiscal changes, It is, for example, high time that a European Company Law should see the light of day. Similarly, a Community Corporation Tax Directive should be accepted.

More strictly technical problems which deserve further study are the question of the definition of the money supply at a Community level and the question of the size and maturity of the national debt in different Member States.

The Regional Question.

To date, the EMS has been successful. Therefore, some Europeans would be right to examine the possibility of eventually transforming the present System into a full economic and monetary union. Certainly, when one examines the table showing the most recent levels of inflation it is clear that there is a number of low inflation countries which could be candidates for a more accelerated move towards integration. However, before such a move could be envisaged, something quite radical would have to be done about the regional questions. If this problem is not resolved, even some of the countries which may appear to be technically ready for a more advanced move towards further integration would not consent to such a move. So, what is to be done? Basically, alas, it is a question of resources, yes, resources. If countries will not agree to an increase in the Community's own resources, then some of those currently devoted to agriculture, for example, will have to be moved towards industrial/technological development and the regions.

At a more institutional level, the author has given his support to the proposal made over ten years ago by his old friend, Giovanni Magnifico, for the creation of a European Regional Bank which would partly complement the excellent work already undertaken by the European Investment Bank (E.I.B.).

What is Likely to Happen.

So, what, in reality, is likely to happen? The Governments of the Member States are almost certain to try to resist progress - certainly they will refuse to create any more "official" ECU's through the "revolving" Swap Arrangements. Further, they are likely to use the most facetious arguments and excuses for not creating a "Real" Fund. But, since business is business and the commercial ECU is a success and continues to grow, then, some arrangements just have to be made. To give one precise example, it is most probable that ECU-denominated travellers-cheques will be issued before the end of this year. Similarly, ECU bank deposits - like international ECU commercial bonds - will continue to grow in size. Therefore, in the face of the refusal of the B.I.S. to accept any more Community chores, the Community will have to make some arrangements - will, in fact, have to finally accept a real responsibility for the active total (and not, as at present, for the partial) management of the EMS. Something will just have to happen. Perhaps the commercial banks will set up their own clearing union ... may be this could be the best solution of all.

According to present trends within the Community and the confusion russrounding the US Dollar and the American banking system, the ECU will continue its present successful development and the demand for it is likely to increase at an international level. It will be this ever-increasing success of the ECU which is likely to be an integrating factor within the Community, and, which, in turn, is likely to transform the EMS into something more than its present state as a de-facto monetary union. Perhaps, it will not be transformed into a full EMU for a number of years - though, here, a Community of Member States developing at different speeds is a distinct possibility. This eventuality is likely to become more real with the prospective membership of Portugal and Spain. Whatever happens, the EMS will most probably continue its record as the only real success story of the European Economic Community since the First Enlargement.

Conclusions : Notes.

1. See: Pascal Salin, "European Monetary Unity : For Whose Benefit?" The Ipswich Press, 1980.

2. According to the Financial Times (15. May 1984), a Community working party was on the point of sending detailed proposals to the BIS for the creation of a two-tier ECU clearing union - within the framework of the BIS.

APPENDIX I

The "Snake" System : Record.

1971	
August 15.	Suspension of dollar convertibility to gold.
December 19.	Smithsonian Agreement : Return to fixed parities for IMF currencies : band of 4.5 per cent allowed for the dollar.
1972	
March 21.	Resolution of the Council of the European Communities proposing the "Snake" of the Community currencies (a band of fluctuation of 2.25 per cent) in the dollar tunnel (a band of 4.5 per cent).
April 10.	Basel Agreement between EEC central banks to implement the Resolution of 21 March.
April 24.	Implementation of Basel Agreement. Participating countries: Belgium, France, Germany (West), Italy, Luxembourg and The Netherlands.
May 1.	Pound Sterling, Irish Pound and the Danish Krone join the "Snake" Arrangement.
May 23.	The Norwegian Krone is associated with the "Snake".
June 23.	Britain and Ireland leave the "Snake".
June 27.	Denmark leaves the "Snake".
October 10.	Denmark rejoins the "Snake".
1973	
February 13.	Italy leaves the "Snake".
March 12.	The Deutsche Mark is revalued 3 per cent vis-à-vis the European Monetary Unit of Account (EMUA). The participating Member States in the "Snake" organise a joint float against the U.S. Dollar.
March 14.	The Swedish Krona is associated with the "Snake".

June 29.	The Deutsche Mark is revalued 5.5 per cent against the EMUA.
September 17.	The Dutch Guilder is revalued 5 per cent against the EMUA.
November 16.	The Norwegian Krone is revalued 5 per cent against the EMUA.

<u>1974</u>.

January 19.	France leaves the "Snake".

<u>1975</u>

July 10.	France returns to the "Snake".

<u>1976</u>

March 15.	France again leaves the "Snake".
October 17.	Special Realignment (the "Frankfurt" one) of exchange rates against the EMUA. Deutsche Mark revalued 2 per cent; Danish Krone devalued 4 per cent; Norwegian Krone and Swedish Krona devalued 1 per cent.

<u>1977</u>.

April 1.	Devaluations against the EMUA. Swedish Krona : 6 per cent. Danish and Norwegian Kroner : 3 per cent.
August 28.	Sweden leaves the "Snake". Devaluations against the EMUA of 5 per cent for the Danish and Norwegian Kroner.

<u>1978</u>

February 13.	Devaluation of 8 per cent of the Norwegian Krone against the EMUA.
October 17.	Revaluations against the EMUA. Deutsche Mark : 4 per cent; Dutch Guilder and Belgian Frans : 2 per cent.
December 4/5	Meeting of the Council of Ministers in Brussels : adoption of Resolution establishing the EMS.
December 12.	Norway leaves the "Snake" System.

<u>1979</u>

March 13. Governors of Central Banks and Board of Governers of EFMC sign instruments implementing the EMS.

Source: Commission of the European Communities.

APPENDIX II

The European Monetary System : Record.

1979

March 13.	Introduction of the EMS.
September 23.	Adjustments within the EMS. (1) a 5% re-evaluation of the Deutsche Mark vis-à-vis the Danish Crown, and (2) a 2% re-evaluation of the Deutsche Mark vis-à-vis the Belgian, French and Luxembourg Francs, the Dutch Guilder, the Italian Lira and the Irish Pound.

1980

November 27.	A 5% devaluation of the Danish Crown within the EMS.

1981

March 23.	A 6% devaluation of the Italian Lira within the EMS
October 4.	A 5½% revaluation of the Deutsche Mark and the Dutch Guilder. A 3½% devaluation of the French Franc and the Italian Lira within the EMS

1982

February 21.	A 8½% devaluation of the Belgian Franc. A 3% devaluation of the Danish Crown within the EMS.
June 12.	A 4.25% revaluation of the Deutsche Mark and the Dutch Guilder. A 5.75% devaluation of the French Franc. A 2.75% devaluation of the Italian Lira - all within the EMS.

1983

March 21.	A 5.5% revaluation of the Deutsche Mark

A 3.5% revaluation of the Dutch Guilder.
A 2.5% revaluation of the Danish Krone.
A 1.5% revaluation of the Belgian/Luxemb. Franc.
A 2.5% devaluation of the French Franc and the Italian Lira.
A 3.5% devaluation of the Irish Pound.

1985. On 21 July:

A 6% devaluation of the Italian Lira.
A 2% revaluation of the Deutsche Mark, the Dutch Guilder, the Danish Krone, the Belgian/ Luxembourg Franc, the French Franc and the Irish Pound.

1986. On 7 April:

A 3% revaluation of the Deutsche Mark. and the Dutch Guilder.
A 1% revaluation of the Belgian/Luxemb. Franc and the Danish Krone.
A 3% devaluation of the French Franc.

(Reproduced in part from: P.Coffey, "Main Economic Policies of the EEC", Nijhoff, 1983).

APPENDIX III

Financial Integration : Communication from the Commission to the Council, 20. April 1983.

Concerned at the lack of integration that had been achieved between the Community's capital markets, the Commission sent a communication to the Council of Ministers on 20. April 1983, COM (83) 207 final, in which the need to relaunch efforts in the direction of financial integration was stressed. Similarly, the Commission made practical proposals for a "realistic process of financial integration". In view of the importance of this document, the author has decided to highlight and examine its most important points - rather than making a direct recapitulation of the communication.

The Background.

The Commission's cry of alarm stems from the fact that capital movements within the Community are less free now than they were in the 1960's. As support for this assertion, France, Italy, Ireland and Denmark are listed as countries maintaining controls for most capital movements. In contrast, four countries have lifted controls on all capital transactions, Germany, the United Kingdom, Belgium and Luxembourg (though a dual capital market exists in the latter two countries).
The reason for this state of affairs is the misuse by Member States of articles 73 and 108 of the Treaty of Rome as measures of more general economic policy rather than as exceptional ones. Thus, there is a frequent and general recourse to the use of the safeguard clauses as contained in the 1960 and 1962 Council Directives aiming at the implementation of article 67 of the Treaty of Rome.
To the author, the Commission correctly reminds the Council that Community financial instruments (apart from inter-central bank credit mechanisms) have indeed been devised precisely in order to help countries facing temporary balance-of-payments and similar difficulties. These instruments are the medium-term financial assistance and the Community loans mechanism. However, this support is "conditional upon observence

by the recipient countries of certain jointly agreed economic policy conditions. Thus, in these last words lies the reason why Member States prefer the apparently easier (at least in the short term) expedient of imposing controls over capital movements.

To the Commission, however, the present situation is a negative one since Member States are imposing controls on a regular basis whereas they should be used as a last resort. In contrast, the large amount of Community financial resources have not been used since 1977.

The Desirability of Financial Integration.

To the Commission, unless capital movements are freed among the Community's Member States, then firms will not be able to exploit economies of scale associated with a large single integrated market. In contrast, financial costs absorbe a growing proportion of firms' gross operating surpluses. These costs could be reduced if greater competition existed in the Common Market.

The Commission also suggests that the following advantages would result from a freeing of capital movements and integration of capital markets:

(i) a more easy and "direct tapping of European savings would make for more effective re-structuring of the Community economy". To support this claim, the observation is made that in 1980, gross savings in the EEC amounted to 430.000 million ECU's - compared with only 340.000 million ECU's in the United States. Yet, very little of this total is tapped by national financial markets.

(ii) There exists among Community financial centres (notably in London and Luxembourg) very important intermediary services and expertise. These could be used by a Community system. Unfortunately, at the present time, these centres are used for the Euromarkets, which, so the Commission claims, tend to be destabilising.

The Commission's "Practical Proposals for a Realistic Process of Financial Integration".

The Commission has made a number of proposals for facilitating fanancial integration which they call "specific initiatives". These initiatives are:

(i) the gradual dismantling of partitions between capital markets. In

In this context, the Commission believes that the Community should concentrate on the establishment of a European equity capital market. In the same vein, there should be no discrimination between the securities of national companies and those of the companies of the other Member States.

(ii) According to the directive of 12.December 1977, rules were laid down for the co-ordination of national laws regarding the establishment of financial agencies and branches. In brief, the Commission is calling for a "more unified network of financial services".

(iii) The Commission also calls for a strengthening of the links between national stock exchange markets in order to more easily pool existing resources and end compartimentalisations. One way of facilitating this task would be to remove restrictions on the listing of foreign shares. Also (as is suggested on the draft Directive on indirect taxation on securities' transactions) double taxation should be stopped.

(iv) Encouragement should be given to collective investment undertakings for transferable securities.

New Instruments for Tapping Savings in the Community

In its call for the development of new financial instruments, the Commission stated its intention of taking action in three ways:

(i) the encouragement of closer collaboration between medium - and long-term credit institutions on programmes/projects of common interest. Here, a novel proposal was that of launching a programme of unified loans simultaneously on the markets of Member States.

(ii) The establishment of collective investment undertakings for industrial purposes.

(iii) The authorisation for housing credit establishments to place their mortgage bonds ("up to a certain ceiling") in other Member States.

In contrast with the numerous afore-enumerated calls made by the Commission for a greater liberalisation of capital movements between the Member States of the Community, it made a call for a greater control over capital movements between the EEC and the rest of the world and more specifically for the co-ordination of the foreign borrowing policies of the Member States.

Again, a counterbalance or logical ingredient to such a move is the establishment of monetary stability within the Common Market itself. To this end, the Community re-iterates its proposal for a "Directive on banking supervision on a consolidated basis".

In its overall conclusion, the Commission repeated its call for the promotion of the use of the ECU, its recognition as a foreign currency and for a privileged treatment for financial transactions conducted in ECU's.

APPENDIX IV.

Communication from the EC Commission to the Council (*)

The promotion of the international role of the ECU.

1. The conclusions of the Presidency of the European Council in Bremen stipulated, in paragraph 1 of the annex, that the ECU should be at the heart of the EMS; the Resolution of the Brussels European Council foresaw in paragraph 2.7. that the ECU would be at the centre of the EMS. Both national and Community authorities have repeatedly stressed the need to develop the role and usage of the ECU, both public and private. This Communication deals only with the private use of the ECU.

2. The private use of the ECU, which commenced only two years ago, has taken off rapidly; it is a method of invoicing which is becoming more and more widespread, particularly in the case of multi-national companies; its role as a means of payment should be reinforced by a better exploitation of the existing usage possibilities; it is, in some Member States, an increasingly important instrument for the denomitation of financial investment; finally, the volume of ECU-denominated issues makes it the third most used currency, after the dollar and the DM, for the floating of bonds on the international markets.

3. Nevertheless, steps must be taken to secure the development of the private use of the ECU; such a development is, in fact, a necessary means of reinforcing the European monetary identity, internal and external

a) Increased use of the ECU would constitute, first of all, an important element in a renewed movement towards internal financial integration in the Community; it is clear that the ECU, the expression of a monetary zone in formation, cannot continue to be subject, within the EEC, to those restrictions which in some Member States are imposed on foreign currencies.

b) It is even more necessary that the development of the ECU in international markets should permit the progressive distributions over all Community currencies of capital movements which, at present, take place between, on the one hand, the dollar, and, on the other, those European monies which are alternatives to the US currency. The enlargement of the ECU-market would, moreover, bring about a better equilibrium between

the source of funds, at present very limited geographically, and their use.
4. The Commission proposes that the promotion of the role of the private ECU should take place under three main headings:

a) Status of the ECU.

The ECU is treated differently, de facto or de jure, in the various Member States. This differentiation range from a total ban to complete freedom, encompassing formulae which, while not forbidding operations in ECU's, nevertheless result in increased costs for such operations.

The Commission proposes that the necessary measures be taken, in all Member States, to accord foreign currency status to the ECU. To this end, it proposes that the Council adopt the draft Resolution attached in Annex 1.

b) Use of the ECU.

Transactions in ECU-denominated bonds must be liberalised, that is to say, made accessible to Community residents under normal conditions. This privileged access to the ECU-market by residents requires, on the part of several Member States, derogations from their exchange control laws.

The Commission has made proposals in this respect in its Communication of financial integration.

c) Protection of the ECU trademark.

Although the banking profession follow uniform procedures when referring to the ECU, private initiatives taken in the context of national regulations, often designed for other purposes, risk giving rise to divergent applications of the ECU and, therefore, prejudicing its development.

The Commission will, therefore, propose, when all Member States have recognised the ECU as a foreign currency, a document which will constitute a reference text for the ECU. This text will define the status of the ECU and clearly state the rules which users will have to follow; it will reproduce the various texts regarding the definition of the ECU, refer to its recognition by the Member States and assure the protection of the ECU trademark.

Annex 1

The Commission requests the Council and the Member States to adopt the following draft Resolution regarding the ECU:

"The Council considers that the development of the role of the ECU is

an important part of the internal consolidation of the EMS and the affirmation of its external role.
It has noted the Communication of the Commission in the matter, and, particularly, the suggestions made to facilitate the treatment and promotion of the use of the ECU. The relevant authorities have expressed their intention to take all the measures necessary to ensure that the ECU operations are treated, in the context of their internal regulations, as foreign currency operations".

(*)
COM (83) 274 final -
Brussels, 24 May 1983.

APPENDIX No. V

The Herman *) Report.

InFebruary 1984, the European Parliament adopted the Herman Report on the European Monetary System.

In general, this Report underlined the good performance of the EMS, but made four criticisms about it. These were:

1) the creation of ECU's seems too automatic, being unconnected with the financial needs of the Member States.
2) the lack of coordination of the monetary policies vis-à-vis third countries' currencies;
3) the low degree of acceptability and negotiability of the ECU and its non-convertibility;
4) the lack of convergence towards the goal of internal stability of the EMS.

The Report made the following four proposals for improving the System:

1) The setting up of an "alarm system" based on indicators such as wages, public deficits, interest rates, balance of payments, inflation rates.
   Member States should follow the EC Commission recommendations for the adoption of corrective policies, otherwise they would be deprived of some EEC financings.
2) The role of the FECOM should be strengthened by means of the assumption of new responsibilities, such as the management of already existing credit systems, the coordination of the policies towards the US dollar and, in a further stage, its responsibility as the central bank of the ECU.
3) The private use of the ECU should be developed; all Member States

*) This was the surname of the former Belgian Minister for Lconomic Affairs.

should give the ECU full recognition as a convertible currency. The ECU should be officially quoted on all the Stock Exchanges of EEC countries, and transactions on bonds denominated in ECU should be freely accessible to all European residents. Besides, the minting of a coin of 1 ECU is recommended and a competition for a symbol for the ECU should be lainched.

4) The pound should quickly enter the EMS.

Appendix VI

The Basic Structure of Banking in EEC Countries.

In Part Four of this book, the author examined the influence of the State on commercial banks in Common Market countries. In this appendix, the intention is to provide very basic structural and descriptive information about central banks and the commercial banking systems in the EEC.

The Central Bank.

West Germany.

The Bundesbank (the West German Central Bank) is fully independent. This is really most important. According to the country's constitution, the Bundesbank is endowed with the fundamental responsibility for control over credit policy and for maintaining the stability of the currency (in reality, the value of the Deutsche Mark).

In order to underline this independence, it is interesting to note that while Government Ministers may, by right, participate in the meetings of the Bundesbank's Central Council (without voting rights), the President of the Bundesbank, must, by law, be invited to participate in all meetings of the Council of Ministers at which questions related to monetary policy are discussed.

France.

The Banque de France "receives from the State the general task of supervising the currency and credit policy". This basic legal preamble clearly explains the position of the French Central Bank vis-à-vis the State. This position is further underlined by the responsibility of the National Credit Council in controlling credit. The President of this Council is the Finance Minister.

The United Kingdom.

The Bank of England occupies a place, regarding its independence vis-à-vis the State, somewhere between that of the Bundesbank and the Banque de France. The British Central Bank does possess a high degree of responsibility for monetary policy, and, obviously, for maintaining the value of the Pound Sterling. The author would observe that the management of national monetary policy in the United Kingdom is one of co-responsibility between the Treasury and the Bank of England. In the last resort, the Treasury may give directives to the Bank - but this is normally never done.

The Netherlands.

In the Netherlands, the Nederlandse Bank, the Dutch Central Bank, possesses a high degree of independence and responsibility in the application of the country's monetary policy and in maintaining the stability of the currency. In the last resort, the Finance Minister may have the last word - but recourse to such an eventuality almost never takes place.

Italy.

Although, in Italy, national monetary policy is the joint responsibility of the Interministerial Committee for Credit and Savings (composed of representatives of the Treasury, the Banca d'Italia and the Ministry of Finance), the Governor of Italy's Central Bank does enjoy great independence and much freedom of action. Also, as a result of Italy's economic and political problems since the end of the Second World War - together with the great professional competence and integrity of successive Governors of the Banca d'Italia - this position has assumed a degree of influence and importance which was not constitutionally foreseen.

Belgium

Some experts consider monetary policy in Belgium to be one of " mutual consent" between financial intermediaries and the public authorities - under the ambrella of a special committee created for this purpose. However, the three major institutions concerned are the National Bank of Belgium (Banque Nationale de Belgique), the Banking Commission (Commission Bancaire) and the Finance Ministry. In this triumvirate, the principle role of the National Bank (apart from the traditional of one issuing banknotes, controlling credit and banker to the State) is that of initiating proposals concerning monetary policy. However, it is the Banking Commission (an independent organ) which is responsible for supervising the banks.

Denmark

The Danmarks Nationalbank, the Danish Central Bank, is the principal monetary authority of the country. As such, it is more independent and possesses greater responsibility than its Belgian counterpart. Together with the Government, the Danish Central Bank shares responsibility for the country's monetary policy.

Ireland

According to the Central Bank Act of 1942, the Central Bank of Ireland is responsible for maintaining the stability of the currency and supervising banks and credit. However, according to the same Act, it is the finance minister who has the last word (where necessary) concerning the Bank's responsibilities.

Luxembourg

Since 1. June, 1983, the Institut Monétaire Luxembourgeois (Luxembourg Monetary Institute) came into being. This institute is endowed with the powers of a central monetary authority for Luxembourg and brings together a number of functions formerly performed by other bodies. Legally, the new Institute is the successor to the former Luxembourg Banking Commissioner. The Luxembourg Monetary Institute does, however, enjoy much wider powers than its predecessor.

The Author's Observations

This overview shows that there exists a considerable difference between the different central banks in the Community regarding the degree of independence and responsibility which they enjoy.

At one end of the scale there is the Bundesbank, the West German Central Bank, which is, for all intents and pusposes, completely independent.

At the other extreme, there are the Banque de France, Banque Nationale de Belgique and the General Bank of State of Luxembourg. In the case of the last two countries, the Central Bank is not even responsible for supervising banks - this role vested in special banking commissions.

The other central banks fall somewhere in between these two extremes with those of the Netherlands, Denmark and Ireland enjoying quite a high degree of independence.

These important differences between the central banks in the Common Market countries give some indication of the major problems which the Community faces when trying to agree on a plan for a "real" European Monetary Fund. In this context, it is perfectly understandable that the Bundesbank and the Germans in general are, in principle, unwilling to accept anything less than a completely independent fully fledged European Central Bank.

Commercial Banking Structures

The general trend in commercial banking in the Common Market is towards concentration and to the transformation of specialised banks into the German type of "department store" bank - offering many diverse services.

Although it is very difficult to obtain up-to-date reliable fugures about the degree of concentration in the commercial banking sector of the Community, the following figures for 1975 give some clear indication of the trends:

West Germany

Major commercial banks: responsible for under 45 per cent of total business.

United Kingdom

The "Big Four" London clearing banks collected 75 per cent of all deposits.

France

The main deposit banks collected over 50 per cent of total deposits.

Italy

The top nine commercial banks were responsible for approximately 50 per cent of total business.

The Netherlands

The top two commercial banks were responsible for 35 per cent of total business.

Belgium

The top two commercial banks were responsible for about 32 per cent of total business.

The Types of Commercial Banks

West Germany

Despite the author's apparent obsession with the idea of the German "department store" type of bank, there exists a surprising variety of banks in the country, and, the big well-known commercial banks (in

1975) were responsible for under 45 per cent (see above) of total business in the country. In reality, there are four major types of banks in West Germany, the big commercial banks, the savings banks, the regional ones and the specialist banks.

France

Until the banking reforms of 1966-67 banking was rigidly and carefully divided into separate compartments. Although the different kinds of banks do still exist, they are now allowed to undertake different kinds of business. The most notable example here is that of the Crédit Agricole (the farmers' bank - perhaps the largest national commercial bank in the world) which now offers package holidays as well as mortgages. The different types of banks in France are the deposit banks, the merchant/business banks (banques d'affaires), the credit banks and the public or semi-public institutions.

United Kingdom

Although there are a number of different specialised banks and institutions in Britain, the whole system is very much denominated by the clearing or deposit banks which hold over 90 per cent of all deposits. Apart from these huge deposit banks, the British financial scene is noted for such specialised institutes as acceptance houses and the merchant banks (the latter specialising in international trade). The other important financial institutes are the building societies and the savings banks. There are, also, many, many branches of foreign banks in the City of London.

Italy

Banking in Italy is regional and to a certain degree specialised in nature. As in France, the major commercial banks are owned by the State.

The different types of banks in Italy are the chartered public banks, the banks of national interest, other commercial banks, co-operative banks and the saving banks.

The Netherlands

The Dutch banking scene is similar to the British one. Thus, as in Britain, in the Netherlands, it is normal for banks to provide finance for business - but not to own business. In the Netherlands there are mainly four different kinds of banks, the commercial banks, agricultural banks, savings banks and central credit institutions.

Belgium

The Belgian banking scene is dominated by the national savings bank and public sector financial intermediaries. Coming behind these institutions - and in third place - are the commercial banks.

Denmark

As in the United Kingdom, the Danish banking scene is dominated by a few big commercial banks. The other important financial institutions are the regional commercial banks and the saving banks.

Ireland

Like Denmark and the United Kingdom, the Irish banking scene is dominated by a few important commercial banks. However, in recent years, a number of financial institutions have grown up which are not "licensed banks" - and which therefore fall outside the jurisdiction of the Central Bank of Ireland.

Luxembourg

The "Luxembourg system is unique in the Community in that the international side is by far the dominant feature. Deposits in Luxembourg Francs account for only 30% of total deposits". *)

Luxembourg, then, offers two major attractions to the non-resident, one is its facility for holding companies (see the 1929 Holding Company Act), the other is the fact that wealth and interest on bank deposits are free of income tax. As a result of these incentives, most banks in Luxembourg are foreign owned.

The Author's Observations

This short overview of the commercial banking scene in the Community indicates that differences still exist in the baning structures among individual countries. At one end of the spectrum as in Britain, Denmark and Italy, the banking scene is dominated by e few commercial banks. At the other end, as in France and Italy, the majority of deposits

*) Quoted from: An Analysis of Banking Structures in the European Community", Banker Research Unit, 1974. The author wishes to acknowledge this publication as a source of some of the material concerning commercial banks in this appendix.

are controlled by nationalised banks. In Belgium, public sector financial intermediaries and the national savings bank dominate the scene. In Italy, banking is regionalised whereas in Luxembourg, it is almost wholly international. The City of London also possesses a strong international presence.

Apart from these (and a growing tendency towards greater concentration) factors, there still exist, in a number of countries, quite different types of specialised financial institutions.
Only in two countries, Luxembourg and Britain, is there a conscious effort to attract foreign banks. This fact, together with the already discussed most recent banking directive, explain the relatively meagre degree of inter-Member State banking penetration hitherto achieved within the EEC. There exists much room for competition.

INDEX

Supplement to the Second Edition.

Introduction

Since the publication of the first edition of this work, a number of changes have taken place within the European Monetary System (EMS). At the very basic level, there have been two currency re-alignments - of which the second one was particularly controversial. Then, the official ECU has been re-structured to allow for the inclusion of the Greek Drachma.

The Commission has made important proposals for strenthening the EMS and Mr. Delors constantly calls for a greater liberalisation of Community Capital Markets. These calls are set against a background of major de-regulation moves in this field in the Netherlands, West Germany and the United Kingdom. Similarly, France has relaxed its exchange controls. All these moves are set against a background of falling levels of inflation and interest rates.

Agreement has finally been reached with the Bank for International Settlements (B.I.S.) to bring on stream a Clearing Union for commercial ECU's in 1987. Although the author would have preferred a transformation of the present embryonic European Fund for Monetary Co-operation into a real "live" Fund (see: proposals earlier in this book), the present agreement will make things somewhat easier for the seven commercial banks [1)]which currently fulfill this role.

Last, but not least, discussion and controversy continues - stronger than ever - over Britain's possible membership of the EMS. Calls for Britain to join are constantly being made by the Commission, the Head of the Bundesbank and the Confederation of British Industry.

The Currency Re-Alignments.

The re-alignment which took place on 20 July 1985, came almost two and-a-half years after the last one and had been anticipated for a number of weeks. It was a necessary adjustment in order to take account of Italy's less than satisfactory economic performance and the more satisfactory results shown by other economies such as that of Belgium.

The re-alignments agreed upon on 6 April, 1986, were, in contrast, quite unexpected, and, to many experts, unnecessary.

Despite the absence of any abnormal pressures on the French Franc on the international money markets in the preceding days, on Thursday, 3 April, the Banque de France ceased to intervene to support the French currency. Simultaneously, the French Authorities asked for the temporary suspension of the EMS - this was done the following day. The reasons for this request were that the French were about to remove a number of controls on capital and monetary movements in and out of France. Thus, they wished to pre-empt any possible speculaticn against their currency.

During the course of the following two days the Finance Ministers of the eight countries participating in the EMS - plus the United Kingdom as an observer - met in the Netherlands to examine the French request for an 8 per cent devaluation vis-à-vis the Deutsche Mark. The subsequent re-adjustments were somewhat less than the French had hoped for.

The New Definition of the ECU Basket.

The Resolution of the Council of Ministers (5. December 1978) which brought into being the EMS did envisage a five yearly re-examination of the composition of the ECU - and - where necessary, a change in the weights of the component currencies. Thus, the time element did make just such a re-examination likely. Also, since the inception of the EMS, there had been a major divergence in the weights of some currencies. At one extreme, the Deutsche Mark had increased to a level of 36.9 per cent of the total ECU component, whilst the French Franc and the Italian Lira had fallen to 16.7 per cent and 7.9 per cent respectively. Also, whilst it had been originally specified that the Greek Drachma would join the ECU Basket by 31 December 1985, it was also laid down that it should join at an earlier date should there be a change in the ECU definition.

Thus, on Sunday, 16 September, 1984, the European Finance Ministers agreed on a new composition of the European Currency Unit (ECU) which came into operation the following day.

The main features of the new composition are the reduction in the share formerly held by the Deutsche Mark, the Dutch Guilder and the Belgian/Luxembourg Franc. In turn, the French Franc, the Italian Lira and the Irish Punt have increased their share. The Pound Sterling and the Danish Kronor remain stable. The Novelty is the participation - for the first time - of the Greek Drachma in the ECU.

Table 12

	The New Composition: as a percentage of the Total.	The New Composition of the EUC: in National Currencies.
Deutsche Mark:	32	0.719
French Franc:	19	1.31
Pound Sterling:	15	0.0878
Italian Lira:	10.2	140
Dutch Guilder:	10.1	0.256
Belgian Franc:	8.2	3.71
Danish Kronor:	2.7	0.219
Greek Drachma:	1.3	1.15
Irish Punt:	1.2	0.00871
Lux. Franc:	0.3	0.16

The redefinition of the ECU was made using the following formula:

$$P_i = \frac{Q_i}{C_i}$$

where:

P_i = weight of currency; Q_i = fixed quantity of currency;
C_i = ECU exchange rate of currency: per ECU.

This recalculation of the ECU did also necessitate a slight change in the individual Divergence thresholds. Thus using the formula: Threshold = 0.75 x $\mathcal{J}^B$ x (1 - P_i) where $\mathcal{J}^B$ = 2.25 for all currencies, 6.0 for the Lira.

P_i = currency weights calculated on the basis of central parities on 18 May 1983 and quantities before and after the review, the following individual divergence thresholds were calculated.

Table 13

New Divergence Threshold %

Currency:	Before Review:	After Review:
DM	± 1.064	± 1.146
FF	± 1.405	± 1.366
HFL	± 1.496	± 1.516
BFR	± 1.545	± 1.543
DKR	± 1.643	± 1.642
LIT	± 4.151	± 4.051
IRL	± 1.670	± 1.667

Source: EEC Commission. Reproduced from: ECU Newsletter No.10, September, 1986.

Despite slight pressures on currency rates two dates prior to and during the day following these changes, the market thereafter remained quiet - suggesting that the changes had been appropriate and had eliminated uncertainty. Furthermore, the ECU market, as shown by the performace of the ECU Bond sector, tended to widen.

Moves Towards an Integrated Capital Market.

Against a background of planned de-regulation moves (1985) in capital markets, for 1986 in the Netherlands (now implemented) and in West Germany and the United Kingdom (presently in the course of implementation)) - and with the recent relaxation of exchange controls by France, the Commission - and notably Mr. Delors - has made a series of proposals, which, if adopted, should lead to the creation of an integrated European Capital Market by 1992. The achievement of this aim would be the logical counterpart of the completely free Common Market in goods and services planned for the same year.

In October, 1985, the Commission of the European Communities made a number of proposals for the strengthening of the European Monetary System (hereafter referred to as the EMS). These proposals concerned the inclusion of the System in the Treaty of Rome, the transformation of the present somewhat embryonic European Fund for Monetary Co-operation (hereafter referred to as the EFMC) into a " real" Fund which might become a form of European Central Bank, and a call for Greece and the United Kingdom to become "active" members of the EMS.

The Commission's proposals almost coincided with decisions taken by the Council of Ministers to enable unit trusts based in any one EEC Member State to sell to investors in other Common Market countries (with some reservations expressed by Denmark).

The two directives concerning this decision will become effective in 1989. Also, the Ministers agreed to allow an exchange of ECU's between Community organs and central banks with equivalent third party institutions.

More recently, on 22 May, 1986, Mr. Jacques Delors, the President of the European Commission, announced details of a two phase plan to liberalise all remaining exchange controls on capital movements by 1992. The first phase, which took the form of a draft directive to the Council of Ministers, the following month, formally proposed the scrapping of exchange controls in the Community for dealings in unlisted stocks and shares, floating of new share issues on stock exchanges and long-term trade credits. Such liberalisation moves would be mandatory and not voluntary as at the present time.

In the second phase, all monetary and financial flows in the Community would be liberalised. Thus, EEC nationals would be able to have bank accounts in any Community currency, to save or borrow, or take out a mortgage across national boundaries. Similarly no restrictions on the use of credit cards and Eurocheques would exist.

More immediately, the Commission wishes to influence countries such as France, Italy, Greece and Ireland - as well as Spain and Portugal - not to use exchange rate controls to remedy balance-of-payments problems (unless absolutely necessary). Italy and Ireland still have the right to maintain present exemptions until December 1987. However, since France relaxed its exchange controls in May,

1986, that country no longer needs to use its right of exemption.

The Commission's proposals, if adopted, would imply radical changes for Member States. At the present time, regulations require free movement of capital for the following transactions:

(i) direct investments between Member States;

(ii) dealings in quoted securities;

(iii) trade credits, and,

(iv) personal capital movements - save where exemptions are in force.

Although the new proposals are revolutionarywhen one considers the almost complete lack of progress made since the publication of the Segré Report - already 20 years ago - they have been made against a background of de-regulation in a number of Member States. Also, as levels of inflation and interest rates fall and tend to converge and exchange rate speculation is reduced, individual Community countries have less need to impose exchange rate controls. Thus, for the first time in twenty years, the outlook for the achievement of a European Capital Market seems to be realistically positive.

The Clearing Union

Following long and protracted negotiations, the ECU Banking Association (EBA) and the Bank for International Settlements (BIS), signed an agreement, in Paris, on 21 March, 1986, for the setting-up of an ECU clearing system, which, after an initial trial period will come into force early in 1987.

In view of the very great increase in the use of commercial ECU's, it has long since been clear that the original five commercial banks (extended on 1 November 1985 to seven [1]) could no longer play the role of a clearing union. Hence, as early as 1982, the European Commission had initiated the setting-up of a working-party to study the possibility of setting-up such a union. Subsequently, in 1985, the EBA was created and it is this organisation (which, in 1986, includes 58 members plus the Groupement des Caisses

D'Épargne de la Communauté Économique Européenne as a correspondent member) which has signed the ECU Clearing Union Agreement with the B.I.S. and with Swift [2] which will act as the technical agent.

The fact that the Community will, as from January 1987, have access to a ECU Clearing Union can be regarded as an improvement for the EMS. To the author it is also a disappointment because this creation presented the EEC with a golden opportunity to transform the present dodo-like European Fund for Monetary Co-operation into a real live body which could have acted as a clearing union for commercial ECU's, the depositary and creator of Community credits, the organisor of any future official swaps of ECU's and the EEC's accounting agent for ECU's. Instead, the clearing union role - like that of the agent for ECU credits - is given to the B.I.S. - a prestigious international organisation which is not even situated in an EEC country. Despite the present disappointment the author believes that the increasing success of the EMS, the greater use of the ECU and the further integration of the Community will make the creation of a real live Community Fund or Central Bank indispensable.

Britain's Membership of the EMS.

The controversy over Britain's possible membership of the EMS has raged even more furiously since the publication of the first edition of this work.

At one extreme, organisations and personalities both inside and outside the United Kingdom have made regular calls for Britain to join the System. At the other extreme, two recent articles, in the Financial Times, written by the very dissimilar Samuel Brittan [3] and Bryan Gould [4], urge extreme caution before taking such a step. In fact, the latter writer, like the Labour Party which he represents, is formally opposed to British membership.

Situated somewhat more in the middle of the discussion, the House of Lords Select Committee on the European Communitues [5] does give the impression that British room for manoeuvre in the field of economic policy would be circumscribed as a member of the System.

In contrast, both the London Business School [6] and the Federal Trust [7] believe that membership would lead to a greater deal of exchange rate stability. The former report considers that inflation would be lowered if the exchange rate of the Pound Sterling were linked to that of the Deutsche Mark.

All these arguments lead one to ask the basic question, what are British economic and monetary policy aims and would membership of the EMS help Britain to achieve them? As has already been observed in the original text of this work, all West European countries, including Britain, have, for the first time in decades, opted for the same public economic policy goal, i.e. the control of inflation. In the case of some countries - notably France and Belgium - the national authorities believe that membership of the EMS does help them to control inflation because if they do not reduce levels of inflation then unacceptable pressures will build up on their currencies.

In the particular case of Britain, a number of somewhat more complex factors have to be taken into consideration. First, the Pound Sterling is a petro-currency, and consequently tends to display a greater degree of volatility than other European currencies. This would seem to imply that should Britain join the EMS, then, on occasions, the Bank of England may have to intervene massively in the exchange markets in order to maintain the agreed parity of the currency. Also, wide variations in interest rates may be necessary. Both of these factors contain inflationary implications which may also cause unwelcome tensions within the System.

At a fundamental technical level, the question must be asked, what weapons do the British Authorities wish to use in the management of the national economy? During the first years of the Thatcher Administration, much publicity was given to the use of the control of the monetary supply as the main weapon. More recently, one gains the impression, that, having used different definitions for money supply, this weapon is no longer fashionable. Thus, perhaps, greater emphasis should be placed (as is done in West Germany) on the use of exchange rate policy as the principle economic and monetary tool. Here, however, it is essential that Britain try to choose a suitable exchange rate for Sterling particularly vis-à-vis the Deutsche Mark - if she is going to rely on this tool for the management of national economic policy.

Although Britain's room for manoeuvre is likely to be somewhat constrained should she join the EMS, it is likely that the Pound Sterling would be less volatile than hitherto (provided that a realistic exchange rate against the D.M. was chosen) because there would be concerted intervention by all the active members of the System to keep the British currency stable. The question which then remains is whether the price to pay for such stability is too high or not?

The Present and Future of the EMS and the ECU.

Despite the two currency re-adjustments since the publication of the first edition of this work, the EMS can still be said to be an island of stability in a sea of international monetary instability. Also, as levels of inflation and interest rates fall and tend to converge, it seems logical and easier to move on to a more advanced stage of monetary integration. This stage is that of freeing capital movements - an area where so little progress has been made hitherto. Now, as major proposals are made by the Commission and as de-regulation plans in the field of capital markets are implemented by some Community countries, the stage would seem to be set for major progress in freeing and integrating capital markets.

The progress made in the use of the ECU and the outlook for the future, are particularly positive. Since 1985, Euro-cheques denominated in ECU's have been on sale and are widely advertised in a number of Community countries. Even the West German attitude to the ECU is becoming more warm and one can envisage a decision by the Bundesbank to recognise (as is done by all other EEC countries) the ECU as a foreign currency.

Despite the West German attitude, the use of the commercial ECU continues unabated and increases in bank ECU assets and liabilities are observed (see: table 14).

This increased use in commercial ECU's has led to the imminent bringing on stream of an ECU Clearing Union. Although the new arrangement is an improvement on the existing facilities, the author is disappointed that the Community has not gone further. Should, nevertheless, the commercial use of the ECU expand still further and as the Community becomes even more integrated, it will be absolutely necessary to create a "real live" Monetary Fund.

The possibilities for the greater use of the ECU at official and institutional levels have also been increased. Now, central banks may settle up to 100 per cent of debts using ECU's - in contrast with the former limit of 50 per cent. Also, of greater potential at the international level, is the decision taken by the Council of Ministers to allow an exchange of ECU's between Community organs and central banks with equivalent third party institutions.

The author thus considers that the stage is set for a greater use of the ECU by non-Community countries. Notably, agreements could be made with Third World countries where the Community is their main or one of their principal trading partners to quote the prices of commodities in ECU's as well as in U.S. Dollars. A major example of such a possibility is the agreement to settle gas purchases (a new ten year agreement re-negotiated in 1985) made by the Gaz de France with Gasunie (the Netherlands) in ECU's. This agreement had been preceded by one made in the preceding year between a 13-bank committee and the Mexican Government which allowed restructured dollar loans to be partly converted into loans denominated in the banks home currency - including ECU's.

Finally, the question of Britain's membership of the EMS still remains unresolved - largely because of the Pound Sterling's role as a petro-currency together with fears (by Britain) of a possible loss of economic policy freedom. In contrast, Spain has already announced that she will seriously consider joining the EMS at the end of the transitional period when the Spanish currency will become part of the ECU.

In conclusion, the author considers that the changes that have taken place since the publication of the first edition of this work have been important and generally positive. He is optimistic about the future of the EMS and the ECU.

Amsterdam, July, 1986.

Table 14

Assets and Liabilities of Banks in Foreign Currencies

EXTERNAL POSITIONS OF BANKS REPORTING TO THE BIS (currency breakdown- billions of US dollars)

	Foreign currencies									Memorandum items (2) Position vis-à-vis residents
			of which							
	Dollars	Other (1)	D.M.	Swiss Francs	Yen	Sterling	French Francs	Guilders	ECU's	
	Assets									ECU's
1983 Dec.	756.2	265.4	122.2	58.4	17.2	12.4	9.8	10.7	6.9	5.0
1984 March	762.6	285.5	132.5	60.1	18.3	13.6	11.1	10.7	10.1	7.7
June	764.4	272.7	121.4	56.5	21.4	14.3	9.9	10.1	11.9	9.0
Sept.	758.4	262.2	115.8	55.5	20.0	14.0	9.2	9.8	14.5	9.4
Dec.I	778.5	262.7	115.8	51.8	22.1	14.5	8.6	8.9	18.0	10.0
Dec.II	779.0	262.9	115.9	51.9	22.1	14.5	8.5	8.9	18.0	10.2
1985 March	787.1	285.0	117.8	56.6	24.7	20.8	9.2	10.3	23.2	13.9
June	785.6	296.1	120.9	55.8	29.5	20.4	9.6	10.0	26.0	12.8
Sept.	808.2	338.2	140.0	68.2	33.2	20.7	12.9	10.1	31.6	15.0
Dec.	830.7	397.4	162.1	80.9	50.4	23.5	14.4	10.9	38.0	16.2
(3)										
Changes 1984 Q1	6.5	11.2	4.0	1.0	0.6	1.2	0.9	-0.5	3.0	2.5
Q2	1.8	5.7	-1.9	1.0	4.0	1.6	-0.5	0.1	2.5	1.8
Q3	-6.1	8.3	4.1	2.8	-0.7	0.8	0.2	0.5	3.6	1.1
Q4	20.0	9.9	4.5	-1.8	2.5	1.6	-0.4	-0.5	4.1	1.0
1985 Q1	8.0	19.2	-0.1	5.3	2.7	5.2	0.5	1.3	4.7	3.5
Q2	-1.5	6.7	1.8	-2.0	4.5	-1.3	0.3	-0.4	2.5	-1.3
Q3	22.7	2.2	1.5	2.6	-0.7	-1.4	1.9	-1.3	2.4	0.6
Q4	22.4	36.2	10.2	9.3	14.5	2.2	0.7	-	4.0	0.1
	Liabilities									
1983 Dec.	852.7	270.6	113.5	63.9	21.7	14.6	11.3	11.4	7.0	3.0
1984 March	859.8	295.8	129.0	66.5	24.1	15.8	12.9	11.6	10.2	4.5
June	871.3	278.8	119.8	61.4	22.6	16.3	11.6	11.5	10.9	5.6
Sept.	870.1	264.9	110.2	60.2	21.4	16.0	10.3	11.1	13.1	5.7
Dec.I	893.2	264.6	113.0	56.2	21.7	15.9	9.8	10.1	15.9	6.2
Dec.II	896.2	264.6	113.0	56.2	21.7	15.9	9.8	10.1	16.0	6.2
1985 March	903.5	286.7	117.0	62.4	23.3	22.3	10.5	11.5	20.7	9.2
June	896.8	297.2	121.3	61.4	25.7	22.1	10.8	11.3	23.8	9.6
Sept.	914.2	348.8	138.3	77.5	29.5	24.6	15.0	11.6	29.7	12.7
Dec.	937.1	414.0	161.6	90.3	47.5	27.6	17.8	13.4	34.3	13.9
(3)										
Changes 1984 Q1	7.1	16.4	9.7	1.8	1.7	1.3	1.1	-0.4	2.9	1.3
Q2	10.6	2.5	-0.2	-	-0.1	1.5	-0.4	0.8	1.4	1.4
Q3	-1.2	5.1	-0.1	3.0	-0.5	1.0	-0.4	0.4	3.0	0.6
Q4	23.1	9.2	7.1	-2.0	0.7	1.1	-0.2	-0.5	3.3	0.8
1985 Q1	7.3	19.1	1.9	6.8	1.7	5.2	0.5	1.2	4.2	2.8
Q2	-6.8	6.2	3.1	-2.3	2.1	-1.1	0.2	-0.4	2.9	0.3
Q3	17.5	11.0	-0.3	5.4	-	0.7	2.7	-1.3	3.0	1.9
Q4	22.9	41.8	11.6	8.9	15.5	2.2	1.6	0.8	2.4	0.2

(1) For the foreign currency positions of banks in the U.S. no currency breakdown is available.

(2) Banks in Europe, Canada and Japan.

(3) Excludes exchange rate effects.

Source: "International Banking Development Fourth Quarter 1985" BIS, April 1986.

Reproduced from the ECU Newsletter, No.16, April 1986.

NOTES.

1. These are:
   - Banque Bruxelles Lambert.
   - Crédit Lyonnais.
   - Générale Bank SA.
   - Istituto Bancario San Paolo Di Torino.
   - Kredietbank NV (Brussels).
   - Kredietbank SA (Luxembourg).
   - Lloyds Bank PLC.

   This group is known as the Mutual ECU Settlement Account System - MESA.
2. SWIFT : Society for Worldwide Interbank Financial Communications.
3. Samuel Brittan, "Fallacies on EMS Entry", Financial Times, 1 April, 1986.
4. Bryan Gould, "Why Britain must resist the lure of the EMS", Financial Times, 7 May, 1986.
5. House of Lords Select Committee on the European Communities, "European Monetary System", First Report, HMSO, London, 1983
6. The London Business School, Economic Outlook, vol.9, no.10, November 1985, Gower Publishing House, England.
7. Federal Trust, "The Time is Ripe", London, November 1984.

GPSR Compliance

The European Union's (EU) General Product Safety Regulation (GPSR) is a set of rules that requires consumer products to be safe and our obligations to ensure this.

If you have any concerns about our products, you can contact us on ProductSafety@springernature.com

In case Publisher is established outside the EU, the EU authorized representative is:

Springer Nature Customer Service Center GmbH
Europaplatz 3
69115 Heidelberg, Germany

Batch number: 10830943

Printed by Printforce, the Netherlands